LOS ALTOS

FEB 2 0 2002

LOSA

W9-AVL-048

Shades of

The Hidden

Heyday Books

Edited by Kimi Kodani Hill

California

Beauty of Ordinary Life

California's family Album

Introduction by Robert Daseler   Afterword by Carolyn Kozo Cole and Kathy Kobayashi

COVER PHOTO: S-012-683—Los Angeles Public Library. Donor: Florante Peter Ibañez. This was a christening party in honor of the donor's half-sister, Irma. The dancing couple are a brother and sister named Sotello. Wilmington, 1958.

FRONTISPIECE: FOL-98-426—Folsom Public Library. Donor: Marion C. Rader. The Hill family. Left to right: Mr. Bennett; his wife, Marion Caroline Saunders Hill Bennett (also pictured in 33); Mrs. Bennett's granddaughter, Phyllis Marion Hill (the donor's mother), and her parents, Joseph Washington Hill (also pictured in 10) and Mary Clara Azevedo Hill. Folsom, c. 1915.

TITLE PAGE—LEFT: TA001-230—Kern County Library/Taft Branch. Donor: Karen Mitchell. Olive Marie Schmidt and Walter Schmidt Jr. wash the family car. This photo was taken in front of the family's home, which was also a photography shop. The children's father, Walter Schmidt, was a photographer. Taft, 1931.

TITLE PAGE—RIGHT: SSB-0-025—San Bernardino Public Library. Donor: Jack Kitay. Taken in 1956, the photo shows the donor with his grandparents, Lotte and Pete Buncher. Jack's grandparents flew from Pittsburgh for his bar mitzvah at Congregation Emanu-el in San Bernardino. When he started speaking (in Hebrew) he was terrified, but once he got started, "I did okay."

CONTENTS PAGE: TCS1-125—Tulare County Library. Donors: Victor and Vincent Chan. The donors' father, David, an amateur photographer, took this photo of their sister Grace. Visalia, early 1950s.

BACK COVER: SW4-048—Whittier Public Library. The donor, Armando Baeza, shows off his power tools. Whittier, 1991.

© 2001 by Heyday Books

Library of Congress Cataloging-in-Publication Data
Shades of California : the hidden beauty of ordinary life : California's family album / edited by Kimi Kodani Hill ; introduction by Robert Daseler ; afterword by Carolyn Kozo Cole and Kathy Kobayashi.
  p. cm.
ISBN 1-890771-44-9
1. California—Social life and custom—Pictorial works. 2. California—Biography—Pictorial works. 3. Family—California—Pictorial works. 4. Family—California—History—Pictorial works. 5. Minorities—California—Pictorial works. 6. Ethnology—California—Pictorial works. 7. Photograph collections—California. I. Hill, Kimi Kodani.
F862 .S52 2001
979.4—dc21   2001005199

Cover/Interior Design: Dave Bullen
Printing and Binding: Publishers Press, Salt Lake City, UT

Orders, inquiries, and correspondence should be addressed to:
Heyday Books
P. O. Box 9145, Berkeley, CA 94709
(510) 549-3564, Fax (510) 549-1889
www.heydaybooks.com

Printed in the United States of America

10 9 8 7 6 5 4 3 2 1

To the families and their photographers

Contents

A c k n o w l e d g m e n t s

1 [For further information about the photos, refer by number to the endnotes.]

The Shades of California project is an ambitious undertaking by the California State Library to create an archive of California family photographs. It has been a great pleasure to serve as photo editor of this book, which is a selection of images from the Shades of California archive, but in truth I was only one of the many people involved with the "editing."

The first editors were the donors themselves: families tend to preserve the photos that reflect positive moments, and notably absent from these images are the harsh or painful realities of life. A second editing stage occurred at the libraries, when collectors selected photographs from the albums that families brought to them. The selection criteria focused on community and family life, largely within the state but sometimes beyond its borders. Lastly, the assembling of the book was a team effort in which many persons gave input while sharing the excitement of making at least a part of this remarkable collection available to a wider audience.

We would like to extend thanks to the many people, both professionals and volunteers, who worked on this project in its various stages. The inspired staff and volunteers who initiated the Shades of L.A. archive, the predecessor to the state project, were Carolyn Kozo Cole, Kathy Kobayashi, Amy Kitchener, Sojin Kim, and Judith Hopkins, with support from Susan Kent, city librarian of Los Angeles, and the Photo Friends of the Los Angeles Public Library. The initial funding of the Shades of L.A. archive came from the Security Pacific Corporation; Robert Danziger, president of Sunlaw Co-Generation Partners I; the California Council for the Humanities; the Ralph M. Parsons Foundation; and the John Randolph Haynes and Dora Haynes Foundation.

The creation of the Shades of California archive is the achievement of present and former staff of the California State Library: Dr. Kevin Starr (State Librarian), Al Bennett, Robert Daseler, Susan Hildreth, Gary Kurutz, Paul Smith, Mark Parker, and Vickie Lockhart. The consultants hired by the State Library — Sojin Kim, Judith Hopkins, Kathy Kobayashi, Amy Kitchener, Maria Sousa, and Kathryn Morton — and the photographers hired by the State Library — Bob Douglas, Coleman Grimmette, Steve Callis, and Javier Manriquez — as well as the photographers hired by local libraries all contributed expertise. Katherine Cox provided valuable advice, and special recognition goes to Huell Howser for advocating the idea of a statewide Shades project after viewing the L.A. effort.

Essential to the success of this project were the project directors, community coordinators, library staff, and community volunteers who conducted photo collection in their libraries and assisted in the publication of this book. In particular we would like to acknowledge:

Anaheim Public Library: Jane Newell and Joyce Franklin

Berkeley Public Library / South Branch:

  Patty Wong and Jeri Ewart

Corona Public Library: Chris Tina Smith

Escondido Public Library: David Frazee

Folsom Public Library: Kathleen Connors and Jacquie Foster

Fresno County Library: Ray Silvia and Linda Sitterding

Humboldt County Library: Joyce Johnson

Kern County Library / Frazier Park Branch:

  Kristie Coons and Judy Waters

Kern County Library / Taft Branch:

  Kristie Coons and Catherine Edgecomb

Long Beach Public Library: Vivien Reed and Claudine Burnett

Shades of L.A. Archive / Los Angeles Public Library:

  Carolyn Kozo Cole

Madera County Library:

  Linda Sitterding and Steve Fjeldsted

Monterey Public Library: Janis Rodman, Dennis Copeland,

  and Jeanne McCombs

Oakland Public Library: Mae Bolton

Oxnard Public Library: Brenda Crispin

Richmond Public Library: Shelby Sampson

Riverside Public Library: William Swafford

San Bernardino Public Library: Millicent Price

San Bernardino County Library / Yucaipa Branch:

  Cheryl Erickson and Barbara Birabent

San Bernardino County Library / Chino Branch:

  Cheryl Erickson

San Francisco Public Library / Western Addition Branch:

  Susan Goldstein and Patricia Akre

San Francisco Public Library / Mission Branch:

  Susan Goldstein

South San Francisco Public Library:

  Banny Rucker and Linda Saltzer

Sutter County Library: Roxanna Darley and Susan Hoffman

Tulare County Library: Brian Lewis and Nancy Cunha

Watsonville Public Library: Carol Heitzig

Whittier Public Library: Carolyn Rory

Two major financial contributors supported the Shades of California archive project: the Durfee Foundation funded the Library Foundation of Los Angeles from 1997 to 1998; and grants from 1997 to 1999 from the U.S. Institute of Museum and Library Services under the provisions of the Library Services and Technology Act, administered in California by the State Librarian, funded further collecting. The latter also provided funds toward the publication of this book.

Our special thanks to Rina Margolin, Larkin Page-Jacobs, Pete Gianopulos, Ellen Gorelick of the Tulare Historical Museum, Bessie Chin, Richard Hill, Michele McKenzie, Evan Kodani, Elizabeth Kennedy, and Rosie Kennedy for their help, support, and advice. Robert Daseler would like to thank Weston Naef, curator of photographs at the Getty Museum, and Dr. Natalie Cole, assistant director of the California Center for the Book, for their recommendations regarding his introduction.

Our deepest thanks and appreciation to designer David Bullen; to the writers Robert Daseler, Carolyn Kozo Cole, and Kathy Kobayashi; and to the Heyday Books staff: Patricia Wakida, Laura Kennedy, Doug Wakida, Ken Sanderson, Jeannine Gendar, Rebecca LeGates, and Malcolm Margolin—for their invaluable contributions. We greatly appreciate their long hours and unflagging enthusiasm.

Finally, sincerest thanks to the hundreds of donors who generously contributed family photographs to the state collection and to those who further shared their stories for the book. We deeply regret that we could not include all of the photos for which we conducted research (names of donors of photos that appear in this book are in the endnotes). We hope all the donors are as proud of their accomplishment as we are, not only for having created their photographs, but, just as importantly, for having the foresight to preserve them in a public archive.

Kimi Kodani Hill, July 2001

The Hidden California
Robert Daseler

From its infancy in the first half of the nineteenth century, photography promised to reveal an unseen world and open our eyes to a reality that had always been there but had escaped notice until pioneering photographers discovered it. Photography has fulfilled this promise again and again, both in the hands of consummate professionals, such as Carleton Watkins and Ansel Adams, and amateurs, like most of the photographers represented here.

The beauty that resides in these photographs is the abundant, familiar, and, because it is familiar, easily overlooked beauty of ordinary human beings—or since, properly speaking, there is no such creature as an "ordinary human being," it is a kind of beauty that possibly dwells in all of us, no matter how ordinarily plain-featured we are. If this book establishes anything, it is the democracy of beauty, the arguable proposition that it is all around us, all the time. We fail to notice it because we have other things on our minds, but when we linger a moment over a particular photograph, the beauty that escapes notice in the bustle of everyday life shimmers for a second under our eyes, paradoxically more easily noticed when reduced to two dimensions and deprived of color.

The beauty of these pictures is allied to their truthfulness, for with a few exceptions, the photographers represented here know nothing about deception. Unlike commercial photographers, who show us a product in its most attractive or ideal setting, the photographers who made these images are showing us only what they themselves valued, desired, and adored. There is an earnest truthfulness in this endeavor that is, in its own way, far more persuasive than the most accomplished artistry.

This book tells us what we already know but perhaps have not entirely assimilated about life in California: that life on this coast has never resembled its depiction on television and in movies. At any point in the past (and this remains true in the present), the story unfolding in the popular media was extremely selective and partial. Until recently, the Los Angeles Public Library's photo archives reflected this imbalance. Shades of L.A., an inspired project initiated by Carolyn Kozo Cole, was created to document the hidden lives of underrepresented communities in Los Angeles. Since then it has not only remedied the situation but become a testament to L.A.'s—and California's—diverse communities.

The Shades of California project, initiated by State Librarian Kevin Starr, took the Shades of L.A. idea to other communities around the state, with the goal of saving a historical resource of inestimable value before it was lost; all the images now in these archives might otherwise have been scrapped, eventually thrown away or simply misplaced by descendants who no longer knew anything about the people in them. Each library participating in the project, which was funded under the terms of the Library Services and Technology Act, created a new photographic archive, and copies of the contents of the regional archives were deposited at the California State Library as well: approximately six thousand images from more than twenty communities around the state. This book is a selection from that statewide archive.

Robert Daseler is the director of public affairs for the California State Library. For more information on the Shades of L.A. and Shades of California projects, see the Afterword.

2

One afternoon in the spring of 2000, I came more or less by accident to look through a couple of the three-ring binders in which the Shades of California pictures were kept at the California State Library in Sacramento. I was searching for a few pictures I could use in an online newsletter I was preparing, and knowing of the Shades photos, I asked for permission to pore through them. An archaeologist cracking open the tomb of a pharaoh could not have been more breathlessly excited than I was that day. Here was a treasure beyond reckoning, packed up on shelves in a conference room as if it were committee proceedings for a feasibility study. I had a glimpse of something ordinarily hidden: the private lives of people who, in the usual scheme of things, leave scant traces of themselves.

What shall we make of these pictures? Strictly speaking, they tell us very little about the people in them. Though their clothes and hairstyles give us an impression of the period in which they lived or live, and quite often the grouping of three or more figures will suggest a blood relationship between them (and physiognomy may strengthen the suggestion), the bulk of the ambiguity refuses to dissipate. That is part of the appeal of these pictures. Being naturally shy, they invite us to invest ourselves in speculation.

Look, for example, at the pretty girl who resembles an ice cream sundae with whipped cream on top [2]. The elaborate bow on her head must have required very clever hands and a considerable amount of time to contrive. Her entire costume is exquisite, as is she. This is the day of her first communion, and she is filled with the importance of the occasion. She has been preparing for this day for months, and as it is recorded for posterity, she knows she is perfect. Will she ever know such perfection again?

What about the two young ladies in the rumble seat of the roadster [3]? What is the occasion for this picture? Is their father, who peers from the passenger-side window, about to drive them to a party, or—what seems more likely—did the three of them climb into the car especially to be photographed? One is reminded, in looking at this picture, that for much of the twentieth century, the automobile was practically a member of the family, to be cosseted and admired as if it were an exceptional child. And what happened to them, these three people in a car in the third

3

decade of the twentieth century? Learning from the caption that they are members of a prominent San Francisco family may alter the way we look at this picture, just

4

as reading a poet's biography may alter the way we read his poetry, but the essential mystery of the picture remains intact. The fascination of these photographs resides in the images themselves. Other lives remain tantalizingly *other*, beckoning to us from their visible otherness, but remote and unreachable. Photography is the principal theater of this teasing seduction, this siren game.

The young woman in the next photograph [4] is, to my gaze, as alluring as any sullen siren of the silver screen. She stands sideways to the camera, with hardly more of a smile on her lips than La Giaconda. Without knowing a thing about her except what I can see in this picture, I have to assume that the photographer was a man, and that he was in love with her. Why? Because of her smile. It is inviting but still a little reticent, as if she is conscious of the fact that he hopes to appropriate her along with her image.

But already I am projecting a story onto the photograph, which, despite its apparent openness and simplicity, remains indecipherable to anyone unacquainted with its subject. The photographer may actually have been her father or her sister, and the upward curve of her lips may be a response to nothing more amorous than the photographer's entreaty: "Smile!"

There has been no effort made, in selecting pictures for this book, to advance an argument about culture or society in California, or to present Californians in any particular pre-determined light. It is essential, in presenting this material between book covers, not to push meaning at the reader or to impose a point of view that would simplify or encapsulate the experience of exploring this gathering of images. If editor Kimi Kodani Hill had done so, she would almost certainly have muffled the elusive melody of *Shades of California*. It is a faint visual melody that you cannot "hear" if you are consciously listening for it. As your eye moves from picture to picture, face to face, it is as if fingers on a distant piano are attempting a half-remembered musical score. Every three or four bars a note is missed, several notes, but the melody picks itself up and continues, though very faintly. It sounds familiar, and yet you cannot remember when you heard it before. You turn a page and your eye falls on a face, or on a group of faces, and for two bars the melody is almost distinct. You recognize something. No, not a face, but the tone of this particular picture reminds you of a house you visited as a child, with a grandfather clock in the hallway and a murky portrait high on the wall.

A photograph is a sort of insurance policy against oblivion. Nobody wants to be forgotten, to disappear, and when you are happy, you want to preserve your happiness in pictures, so that you can savor it later. You want to capture the evanescence of childhood and the deliquescence of old age. The self-consciousness of these pictures—the act of taking a photograph or posing for one necessarily betrays a degree of self-consciousness—has a peculiar appeal all its own. We see people holding still so that they may be immortalized. The photographer can, for an instant, stop time or at least snatch something from its rapacious maw.

If there is any one quality that dominates the mood of these pictures, it is the sense that the people and things shown were cherished. Whatever else the photographer is doing, he or she is not pursuing a subject as the paparazzi would, or as an ethnographer would, or, with a few exceptions, as an artist would.

These amateur photographers, squinting in harsh daylight or blasting away with flashbulbs indoors, have recorded scenes not for our eyes but their own, and in so doing they have shown us what *they* wanted to remember, and sometimes their pictures reveal more to us than the photographers realized or intended. A few of the children in these pictures look sad or surly. Occasionally the subject of a picture appears to be not entirely in accord with the photographer's purposes.

We cannot forget that photographs indict. They pin us to

a particular place, a hairstyle that has long been outdated, unfashionable clothes, a boyfriend or girlfriend we would prefer to forget, awkward adolescence. The boy at his bureau [5] has a charming, if puzzled, expression on his face. I like the way his undershirt is exposed. I like his short pants, his dark socks. He has arranged his miniature cars very neatly on one shelf, while on the upper shelf he has lined up his toy soldiers. On the wall hangs a pennant for the 1966 Scout-O-Rama. The boy seems poised to say something about his collection of miniature cars, or to apologize for them. He looks anxious and uncertain. The picture, an intruder, delves into his world and the boy seems to want to protect his collections of cars and toy soldiers—and himself—as if incipiently aware of the possibility of being embarrassed by this picture in later years.

Why do people prize their family pictures so highly? In the face of a gathering disaster—a sudden fire or flood, for example, or, in California, an earthquake—people often rush to save their family photographs before other, more conventionally valuable possessions. Family photographs represent everything we can hold of the past, both our own personal past and the deeper past of our parents and grandparents, our uncles and aunts and cousins. Photographs are the vessels of memory, and the details in a photograph convey a sense of the past that is unobtainable from any other source. Photographs are the collective unconscious of our time.

Shades of California represents what we might regard as the hidden California: not the California photographed by visitors, not the California seen in movies, certainly not the California of postcards. It is really not California as anybody would imagine it. It is a world, or many worlds, that people did not want to forget, a world that disappeared as soon as it arrived. Another world has replaced it. It, too, will soon exist only as images.

6

The Photographs

"She always did like to dress up."

Elvira Arvalo

[For further information about the photos, refer by number to the endnotes.]

21

20

22

23

20. Bernaby Guerrero. San Francisco, 1920s. **21.** Margarita Balucas (center) with her daughters, Phyllis and Pilar. Stockton, 1930. **22.** Spanish dancer Amalita De Guerrero. San Francisco, 1897. **23.** Fashion show at Slim Jenkins' night club. Oakland, 1954.

25

27

26

24. David Oliver Martinez (right) and a friend. Oxnard, c. 1920. **25.** Charles E. Hill (right) and a friend. Placerville, c. 1895. **26.** Reuben Schirmer, carpenter, with his cousin, Ralph Leon Wright. Riverside, c. 1925. **27.** Fred Tillman. Berkeley, 1920.

28

29

30

33

34

31

32

35

36

37

38

39

39. Karen Metcalf and Cindy Metcalf get ready for a wedding. South San Francisco, 1982. **40.** Nicholas Edgecomb gets a haircut from Charlene at the Razor's Edge barbershop. Taft, 1989. **41.** Daisy Joe Fung. Visalia, 1915. **42.** The Nunan family, showing off Mama's new haircut. San Francisco, c. 1924.

"Everybody cried when I cut my hair."

Daisy Joe Fung

43

44

43. Mary Slattery. San Francisco, c. 1928. **44.** The Fontana daughters and daughters-in-law at the Riviera Restaurant in San Francisco, c. 1945. **45.** Hilda Antonio, the first African American model for Joseph Magnin. San Francisco, 1920s. **46.** Ethel Fay Mengel. San Francisco, c. 1906. **47.** Letty and Winthrop Guyan Meade at the Pike. Long Beach, c. 1908. **48.** Madeline Coonan Johnson. Eureka, c. 1920.

49

50

51

49. Ann Elizabeth Kashanski in the poppies. Hungry Valley, near Gorman, 1998. **50.** Manuel and Ignacio Aguilera. Durango, Mexico, c. 1905. **51.** Thelma Radden Gibson, Audrey Lucinda Robinson Gibson, Lois E. Oubré Gibson. Oakland, 1918. **52.** Najuma Henderson, Nalungo Connelly, and Ayisha Knight, dressed in their mothers' clothes. Oakland, 1983.

54

55

53

53. Gorlian Xiong, standing in her front yard and holding a traditional musical instrument called a gheng. Long Beach, 1999. **54.** Jennings Glenn Chambers. Whittier. Date unknown. **55.** The Karasawa children. Whittier, 1963. **56.** Sara Gomez's first communion. San Bernardino, 1927. **57.** Greg Giusti in traditional Greek dress. South San Francisco, 1959. **58.** Philip Sloan in San Francisco's Bernal Heights, c. 1957. **59.** Caroline Mota, five years old, and her niece Lala, visiting Colorado from San Francisco, c. 1922. **60.** The Abajian children before coming to America. Kars, Russian Armenia, 1910. **61.** William, John, and Dan O'Donnell. Pismo Beach, 1934. **62.** Elvira Garcia with a Kewpie doll. Long Beach, 1938.

56

57

58

60

59

61

62

63

64

"In those days, we played in the streets."

Lorraine Dillon

65

66

63. Los Altos neighborhood kids. Long Beach, 1969. **64.** Christmas morning. San Francisco, 1922. **65.** The Gang, on Allen Street. Pasadena, 1925. **66.** Two girls and a dog. Place and date unknown.

69

70

71

67. Sharon and Sharman Shimizu. Yuba City, 1958. **68.** Yucaipa Theater, opening day. Yucaipa, 1947. **69.** The Lincoln Traffic Squad at Lincoln Elementary School. Fresno, 1939. **70.** Rose Medina, five years old. Riverside, 1958. **71.** Claremont Middle School science students dissecting squid. Oakland, 1989.

72

72. The second grade of Roosevelt School. Taft, 1937. **73.** Kathleen Rupley's first day of school. Richmond, late 1950s. **74.** Camp Read-A-Lot. Oakland, 1997.
75. Mary Hall (left) and six schoolmates. Taft, c. 1924.

73

74

75

76

77

78

79

76. Mission High School in San Francisco, c. 1946. **77.** The first graduating class of the Colonia School. Oxnard, c. 1890. **78.** Margie and Vivian Cox on their way to Escondido High School from Twin Oaks, c. 1919. **79.** Judith Valles, future mayor of San Bernardino (right, foreground), as a sixteen-year-old high school student. San Bernardino, 1951.

80

81

82

80. Aaron and Drana Brill at their first clothing store. San Bernardino, c. 1938. **81.** Alvah Haworth Wille (at far right) owned the Long Beach Steam Laundry. Long Beach, 1917. **82.** The W. M. Rumsey store at the State Fair in 1936. Sacramento. **83.** Rose Mayes in her record shop. Houston, Texas, 1972. **84.** Tony Ravelli in front of his shoe repair shop. Eureka, late 1920s. **85.** Minucciani Realty. South San Francisco, 1976.

83

84

85

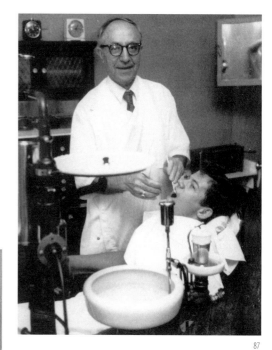

87

86

88

DRILLS *Quality Power Products* YARD and GARDEN TOOLS

Shafers
Henderson Center
HARDWARE

86. Rachel Mendoza, the mayor's secretary, and Bobbie Koenig, council secretary. San Bernardino, c. 1968. **87.** Dentist Mihiran Tevriz with a young patient. Los Angeles, c. 1950. **88.** George Martin watches a co-worker unloading Nehi soda. Fresno, 1930s. **89.** Tony Shafer (center) of Shafer's Hardware. Eureka, c. 1950s.

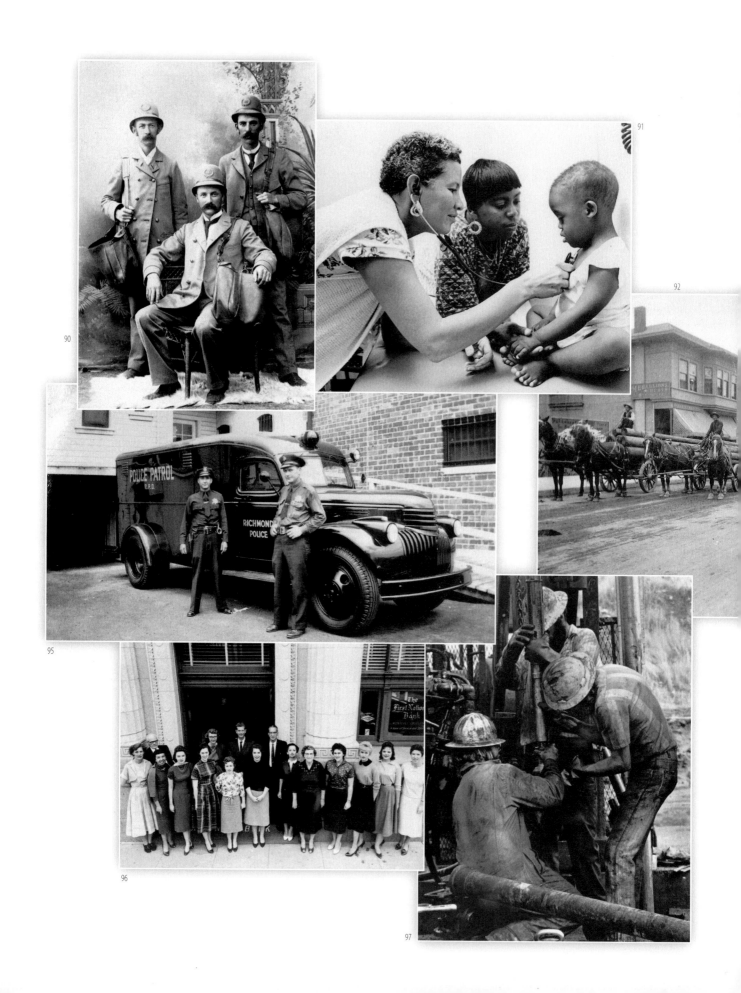

93

94

99

98

100

Sté ANONYME BELGE des PÉTROLES de KERN, Cal.

101

101. Ted King, Paul and Bill Zolnekoff pouring a foundation. Bill Robinson supervises from his lawn chair. Whittier, 1959. **102.** Mary Guerrero Flood in the early 1900s. San Francisco. **103.** Ito Kusumoto at work as a seamstress in the back of her husband's barbershop in Anaheim c. 1919. **104.** Erlinda Felix-Aparicio hangs out the wash. Corona, 1945.

102

103

104

105. The Corona Cubs baseball team, sponsored by Pancho's Garage. Corona, 1940s. **106.** George Linn, catching for his brother Arthur on Marcelli Street. San Francisco, c. 1926.

107

108

107. Fortuna High School basketball team. Eureka, 1912. **108.** Whittier High School songleaders. Whittier, 1947. **109.** Wesley Stewart, nine years old, in his football uniform. Fellows, 1930s. **110.** Michael Hammock (left) playing Little League baseball. Oakland, 1961.

110

109

"If I don't do it now, then forget it!"

Dorothy Henshaw

111

113

114

115

111. Dorothy Henshaw, in a tandem dive on her 66th birthday. Taft, 1993. **112.** Team members in the Long Beach Plaza 8K run wait to hear that they've just won first place. Long Beach, 1989. **113.** Mamma Jane Folgim and friends at the tennis courts, Taft, c. 1920. **114.** Kendo club. Monterey, c. 1930. **115.** "The Strong Men of Kutali" arrive in Los Angeles, c. 1920.

116

117

118

119

120

116. Ladislado Cruz Ortiz and his cat. Place and date unknown.   **117.** Harold Soper and Rascal. Santa Cruz, c. 1900.   **118.** Percy Graves riding the buggy horse. Pleasant Grove, early 1900s.   **119.** Jim Davies, five years old, on the family dairy farm. Mormon Island (near Folsom), c. 1938.   **120.** Kennidi Ricardo with her poodle, Furball. Oakland, 1999.

121

> *"Roy didn't care*
> *who you were."*
>
> Katy Lim

122

121. Roy Rogers and Trigger with local children of Sutter County, 1940s. **122.** John Brownlee on a rented pony. Yuba City, summer of 1937. **123.** Floriza Arvalo, sidesaddle on Catrina. Pico Rivera, 1978. **124.** Derek Morris, age five, on bicycle. Alameda Street, Monterey, 1957.

123

124

125

126

127

125. The Rancho Roundup. Long Beach, c. 1943.   **126.** Mildred O'Guinn on a pony. Oakland, 1940s.   **127.** Abe McFadden, at Garza's Ranch, Carmel Valley, c. 1920.
128. Horses and riders. Santa Cruz, c. 1900.

129

130

129. Salvador Palicte (left) and his friends fixing a car. Santa Maria, 1949.   **130.** The Van Dykes Social Club. Oakland, 1960s.   **131.** Danny Flores and his wife in front of their 1952 Chevrolet Fleetline, "Mexican Graffiti." San Bernardino, 1977.   **132.** Finis Gault, with all his possessions, moving from Springfield, Missouri, to Long Beach, California. On the Grapevine, early twentieth century.

131

132

"Everybody in town knows my car."

Danny Flores

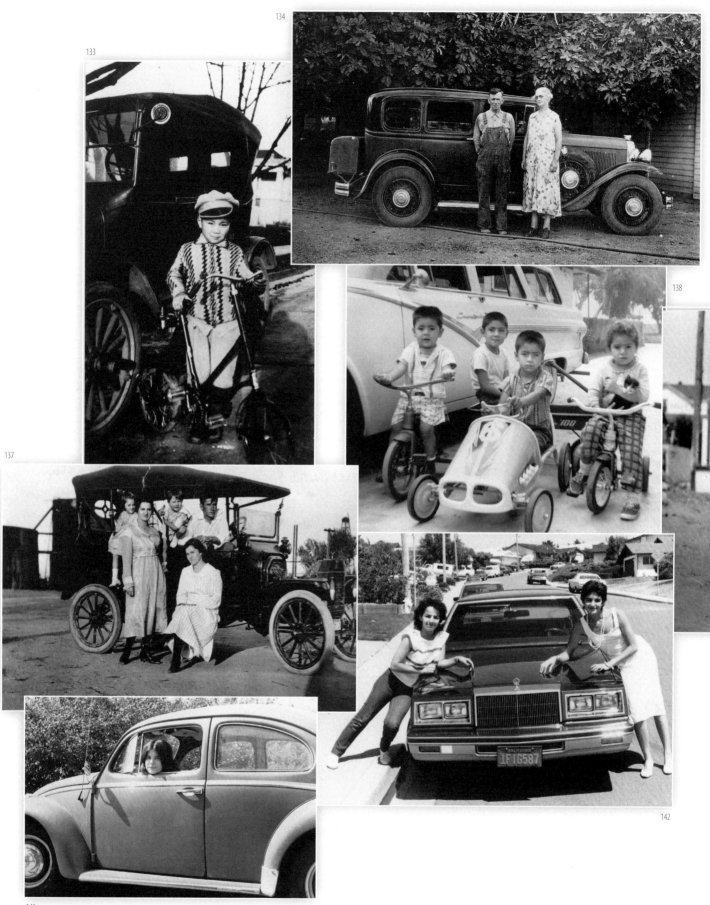

133

134

138

137

142

141

135

136

139

140

143

144

145

146

145. Members of the Tsuneta family at their farm. Dinuba, late 1930s. **146.** Ben Graham on his daughter's bicycle. Monterey, c. 1940. **147.** William Nichols, train engineer, with the dray he used to deliver goods from the train depot to downtown Folsom, c. 1911.

148. The home of Maude Esther Johnson Gibson, shown in the portrait at the far left. Oakland, late 1800s. **149.** The David Green family's housewarming party. San Bernardino, 1953. **150.** New homeowners Gilbert Lopez and daughter Marika Lopez. Riverside, 1995. **151.** Aftermath of the Panorama fire. The man pictured is Bill Becker. San Bernardino, 1980. **152.** Maria Paz Romero's living room. Watsonville, 1970. **153.** Milton and Howard Burdick and an unidentified companion in front of their home. Watsonville, c. 1912.

150

149

152

151

153

154

"Mom won't behave. We can't take her anyplace."

Rose Medina

155

156

154. Barbara Avila Lopez with the Christmas turkey. *Riverside, 1994.* **155.** Henry Gonzales on Santa's lap at the White Front Store. *Anaheim, 1962.* **156.** Christmas 1954. Mary Wiggins, Maxine Lampkin, Estella Rice, Maggie Lampkin. *Oakland.* **157.** The Stewart children at home on Christmas. *Taft, 1958.*

158

159

160

161

162

158. RoseMarie Madrid's first communion. Anaheim, 1964.   **159.** Parviz Gharib-Afshar jumps over the fire at a ceremony on the last day of the Persian year. Los Angeles, 1960.   **160.** Mexican Independence Day at Grape Day Park. Escondido, 1944.   **161.** Easter Sunday. Oakland, 1956.   **162.** Eid-Al-Fitr, celebration of the end of Ramadan. Riverside, c. 1997.

163

164

163. The funeral of baby Tomiko Hirata at Mountain View Cemetery during the influenza epidemic of 1919. San Bernardino.   **164.** The funeral of Tiofolo Estrada's infant son at Holy Cross Cemetery. Anaheim, 1930.   **165.** First communion. Josefina Lozano and Virginia Aguilera. Whittier, c. 1937.

166

167

1943
africa

168

*"They told me how
courageoous I was."*

Ben Chin

166. Albert Grajeda with his buddies. Korea, 1945. **167.** Alvin Cerri, U.S. Navy. South San Francisco, 1942. **168.** Eureka resident Ben Chin, PFC, with the U.S. Army in Africa, c. 1943. **169.** Nadaline and Kay Markich, "lady marines." Riverside, c. 1940. **170.** Glenn Baker, a soldier in the Spanish-American War. San Bernadino c. 1898. **171.** Boy Scouts' Week at Longfellow School. Oakland, 1956.

172

173

174

176

175

177

172. Members of a camera club among Anaheim residents interned at Heart Mountain, Wyoming, c. 1943. **173.** Cambodian students protest the killing of sixteen-year-old Simona Rin in Long Beach, August 1997. **174.** Oscar Rios for Supervisor. Watsonville, 1994. **175.** World War II ends. Gloria Marshaleck, Eleanore Fourie, Violet Sheehan. Yosemite, 1945. **176.** Pickets at Eureka Plywood. Eureka, c. 1954. **177.** The Baeza family watches man land on the moon for the first time. Whittier, 1969.

178. Alice Suyeda, her young son Mike, and his cousin Roy Suyeda reading at home in Ivanhoe, 1948. **179.** Alice Reische. Meridian, 1910. **180.** Raye and Professor Julian Richardson, owners of Marcus Books, with their grandchildren. Oakland, 1983.

179

"It was a wonderful
day of stories."

Kathy Sloane

180

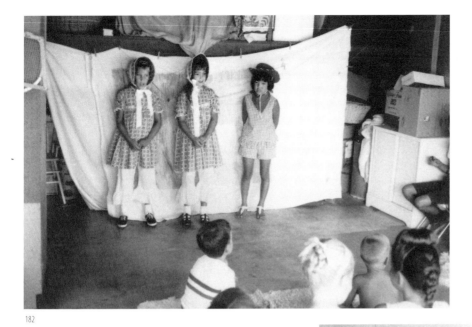

182

183

184

185

181. Family members put on a skit during a party at the Dakessian home in Hollywood, 1963. **182.** We could do our own show! "Garage theater" by neighborhood children. Whittier, 1966. **183.** Teacher Noun Sitandon and her class present a Christmas play at Salesian High School. Richmond, 1996. **184.** A group of friends make a human pyramid at Slick Rock in Three Rivers. Tulare County, late 1920s. **185.** The "Who So Ever Circle" pose for a photographer at the Yosemite Theater in Stockton, 1895.

"Every Thursday was
'Dad's day out.'"

Martha Ann Hilliard

186

187

188

189

190

191

186. John Milton Morton on his 90th birthday at Fisherman's Wharf with his daughter Martha Ann. San Francisco, 1952. **187.** Deputy Sheriff William Tibbet and his son Laurence; Thomas O'Brien, founder of the Lebec Hotel, with his son Thomas. Lebec, c. 1914. **188.** Jose M. Sanchez (left) holds his daughters Lupe (left) and Rita. His brother-in-law Gilbert Fimbrez holds his son Gilbert Jr. Madera, 1936. **189.** Iwao and Jinjiro Masuodo with the day's catch. Yuba City, mid-1950s. **190.** Alicia, Trinidad, and Alfredo Ramirez at the Boardwalk. Santa Cruz, 1971. **191.** Four generations of an Escondido family: Edwin S. Bulen, his son, William (holding his own son, James), and his father, Guy D. Bulen, c. 1947.

192

193

192. Judy White is a bee in the center of a flower float for Carnaval. Richmond, 1995. **193.** The Methodist Church Sunday-school float in Taft's first parade, July 4, 1913. **194.** Tony Ortiz, Nena Aguirre, and Pete Mendoza, with an unidentified child at the Cinco de Mayo parade on Sixth Street. Corona, c. 1945. **195.** Judge Stanley Murray and his granddaughter Shirley Ann Richardson in the Old Timers' Day Parade. Madera, 1940.

194

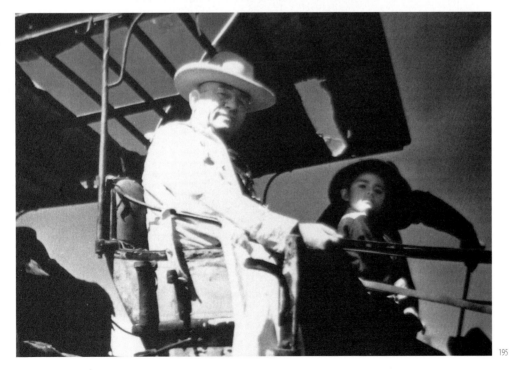

195

196

197

198

199

200

201

196. The Oildorado Day parade. Taft, 1946. **197.** The Oildorado Day World Champion Well Pullers: Pyramid Oil Company crew Billy Hillburn (derrick man), Wally Bingham (pusher), and Matt Bingham (floor man) receive their trophy from Gena Free. Taft, 1965. **198.** Nellie Wong, first Chinese American Raisin Queen for Fresno's Raisin Day, 1924. **199.** Lewis "Bud" Shannon, age 64, "Cowboy of the Year." Madera, 1982. **200.** Vic Borrecco, Ed Bigham, Margo Brown (Miss Kern County 1956) and Mayor Glenn Black in a publicity photo. Taft, 1956. **201.** Cleve Cuddy, Fess Reynolds, and Charles F. Cuddy with their Brahma bulls, which pulled a covered wagon in the Bakersfield centennial parade. Bakersfield, 1965.

202

"Poker was very important
to my family."

Kathleen Rupley

203

204

205

202. Family poker game at the Rupleys'. Richmond, early 1950s. **203.** Charles and Clara Powers pose in a speedboat cutout at the Pike. Long Beach, 1930s.
204. The Pantages, Pantelakis, and Scourkes families on a picnic in the hills to celebrate a baby's christening. San Bruno, c. 1930. **205.** The Lopez family at Knott's
Berry Farm. Buena Park, 1967.

206

207

208

209

210

212

211

206. Alvah Haworth Wille and friends from Spearfish, South Dakota. Long Beach, c. 1920s.   **207.** John and Bob Brownlee with a friend at the swimming hole.
Yuba City, c. 1937.   **208.** Suzanne and Timothy MacConnell splash in a wading pool. Corona, 1985.   **209.** Maggie Wade and a friend. Boyes Hot Springs, early 1900s.
210. Hot tub. Monterey, 1979.   **211.** Sunday school picnic at Aptos Beach. Watsonville, 1910.   **212.** Helen Steinour and Antoinette Starke at Balboa Beach. Riverside,
1935.

213

214

215

216

217

213. The Turner family camping in Yosemite, early 1900s. **214.** Genevieve Deas and her sister Rose Desmond. San Francisco, c. 1900. **215.** Workers and their families enjoy an employee picnic at Uota farm. Ivanhoe, c. 1940. **216.** Sophie Tajima Toriumi with family and friends at Wawona's drive-through tree. Yosemite, 1930s.
217. Esterline Avelino and friends in Yosemite. 1950s.

219

220

218. Farmworker Fausto Romero (right) and a friend. Watsonville, c. 1945. **219.** DeMarcus (surname unknown), Tyrone Peterkin, and Travis Knight. Oakland, 1995.
220. Yow Joe and George Leong, at the Joe family home in Tulare, 1913.

221

222

223

225

226

221. Betty Jean Stevenson and Kashan Thomas behind the El Portal housing project. San Pablo, c. 1954. **222.** Walter and Violetta Deas. San Francisco, 1942.
223. Halloween. Whittier, 1994. **224.** 49th Street kids. San Bernardino, 1967. **225.** Cousins David Leroy Berry and Cecil Neely in front of the Berry home, Upland,
1940s. **226.** Brenda Batchelor and Masako Hirata with a friend in the fifth-grade class at Fourth Street School. San Bernardino, 1925.

227

"The dances all
had live music."

Frances Martinez

228

229

230

231

232

227. "The Highlights" play St. Edward's Hall. Corona, 1949. 228. A group of Armenian performers "jamming" at a party. Los Angeles, c. 1948. 229. "Up with People" performs in Riverside, c. 1981. 230. Mariachi band at a wedding in San Bernardino, 1985. 231. Whittier College Men's Chorus. Whittier, c. 1917. 232. The Fox Theater reopens after post-fire reconstruction. Taft, 1951.

> *"Joseph and I were married."*
>
> Madi Comfort

233

234

233. Von Freeman and his son, Chico Freeman, at Yoshi's Jazz Club. Oakland, 1987. **234.** Woody Herman with the original directors of the Monterey Jazz Festival. Monterey, 1957. **235.** Joseph and Madi Comfort's wedding. Whittier, 1943.

236

237

236. Members of the Cambodian Art Preservation Dance Group before a performance of the wishing dance. Long Beach, 1997. **237.** The Accordion Band on Elm Court in South San Francisco, 1956. **238.** Ballerina kids: Acquanetta and Yvette Maybuce, five and seven years old, in a performance of "Swan Lake." Berkeley, c. 1955. **239.** Folklorico dancers Cecilia Ramirez Furman and Gloria Ramirez Frame. Whittier, c. 1930s. **240.** A dance recital at the Lebec Hotel ballroom. Lebec, c. 1939. **241.** Caroline and George A. Newhall dance at Danny Fontana's baptism in San Francisco, 1955.

243

242

"I didn't think much of him when I met him. He was stuck on hisself."

Roselea Ferguson

242. Gene Sweeney and his girl at the lake. Frazier Park, 1949.   **243.** An unidentified couple with Daisy Joe and W. C. Wyatt at the Prospect Street Fair and Carnival. Tulare, 1913.   **244.** Cleo, Charlie, and Marilyn at the park. Frazier Park, 1947.   **245.** The Van Dykes Social Club. Oakland, 1960s.   **246.** Roselea and Calvin Wayne "C. W." Ferguson at about the time of their fiftieth anniversary. Madera, 1962.

247. Angelo and Ruth Anastasia, Foam Street, Monterey, c. 1946. **248.** George P. Martinez and Irene Martinez in front of the family home. Escondido, c. 1938. **249.** Myron and Virginia Dentadale. Downey, 1976. **250.** Jane and Johnny on Magnolia Street. Oakland, 1950s. **251.** The wedding portrait of Lon Metzger and Mary Nichols. Folsom, 1927.

249

250

251

"My children are very
special and loving children."

Constance Vetter

253

254

255

257

256

252. Vetter family Christmas. South San Francisco, 1994. 253. Snow in San Francisco! Playing in the snow in a Daly City schoolyard, 1962. 254. Irene Canavesio and her niece Angelina Macciro in front of Magnolia School in South San Francisco, c. 1920. 255. Lisa and Yvonne Ng practicing kung fu with their cousin Judy, 1975. Place unknown. 256. Children from the Soboba Reservation in a basketry class. Riverside, 1998. 257. Patrick and Timothy Coe, just before Tim's high school graduation. Richmond, 1976.

258

259

262

263

265

266

260

261

264

267

268

269

270

271

272

270. Helena Julia Neufeld, with her family in front of the family home, Madera, 1945. **271.** Torrie Hill, Mrs. Hill, Dennis White, and Rhonda White. Oakland, c. 1956.
272. Frank and Sally Gonzales with their children at Grandmother's house on Garza Street. Anaheim, 1950.

273

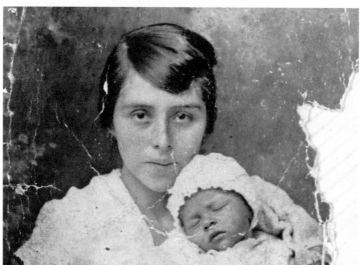

274

276

275

277

273. Honoré Steven holds his daughter, Charmaine, in front of the family's home. Berkeley, 1929. **274.** Tomasina Valdez and her newborn son, George. Douglas, Arizona, 1917. **275.** John Firmalo, Alice (Taone) Firmalo, and their daughter Dorothy. Madera, 1923. **276.** Aunt Kay Wilson holds Jim Bulen, Jr. Escondido, 1976. **277.** Francisca Provencio and her daughter Anetta. Anaheim, c. 1950.

279

278

278. The Bugnatto family on the steps of their Juniper Street house. South San Francisco, 1934. 279. Virginia Rose with her children: Virginia, Mary Ellen, and Richard. Oakland, 1945. 280. Antonia and Cecilio Cervantez with their children Espiridion and Carmen. Place and date unknown. 281. Annie Hayes West Gardiner with her four grandchildren. Fort Tejon, 1890s. 282. Sylvia, Rebecca, and Robert Payne at Sellick Park, South San Francisco, 1985. 283. Gathering wood for the winter at the Cuddy Place. Frazier Park, early 1970s.

280

281

282

283

284

285

286

287

284. Baby Hatsuye Hatakeda with her aunt. Hiroshima Prefecture, Japan, 1920s. **285.** Josephine Purcell, postmistress of Folsom for thirty years, with her four grandchildren. San Francisco, c. 1945. **286.** Sam Reische holding his great-granddaughter, Judy Hale. Meridian, 1939. **287.** Mrs. Delphine Carter at the Black Heritage Celebration, South San Francisco, 1994.

289

288

288. Mary Joe, Jennie Joe, Ling Joe, and Yow Joe. Tulare, 1893. **289.** Mary Joe. San Francisco, 1924. **290.** Mary Joe and members of her family in front of Mary Joe's Café in Tulare. 1945.

"Better to give to all than
to miss one who needs it."

Mary Joe

292

291. The wedding of Alice Lee. Sutter County, 1920s. **292.** Gilbert Fimbrez (center) and Maria Louisa (Sanchez) Fimbrez (on right) on their wedding day. Phoenix, Arizona, 1934.

293

294

295

293. Ramona Ewell throws her bouquet. Long Beach, 1955. **294.** The wedding of Oscar and Juanita Rasul. Yuba City, 1960s. **295.** The three-day wedding celebration of Katherine Kanstanz and David Dauer. Fresno, 1914. **296.** The wedding of Laura Ramirez and John Darius. Whittier, c. 1920.

'95 11 25

297

298

297. Mehendi (henna) hand painting. Riverside, 1996. **298.** Lois E. Oubré Gibson on her wedding day. Oakland, 1941. **299.** Wedding portrait of Lupe Villanueva on her marriage to Carlos Villanueva. Corona, c. 1932. **300.** Mary and Amador Tovar, in their 1948 Chevrolet Fleetline, on their wedding day. Long Beach, 1951.

301

302

301. Early tomatoes and other crops were covered with "hot caps" to protect against a late frost at the Uota farm. Ivanhoe, 1939. **302.** Eldora Botsford feeds her chickens. Taft, c. 1910. **303.** This hay wagon contains oats and vetch, known as "green feed." Humboldt County, c. 1916. **304.** August Santini, six years old, feeds the cows at Arrowhead Dairy. San Bernardino, 1923. **305.** Alice Suyeda and Nancy Morioka picking peas at the Morioka farm near Ivanhoe, c. 1940.

303

304

305

306

307

308

309

Clamming at Clam Beach, California.

306. Minnie Swan and Emil Frey with salmon at Redwood Creek. Humboldt County, 1910. **307.** The commercial fishermen's daily catch at Devil's Gate. Belmont Shore, Long Beach, c. 1900–1907. **308.** Paul Muro after a successful hunting trip near his home. Anaheim, c. 1920s. **309.** Clamming at Clam Beach. Humboldt County, c. 1927.

310

311

312

313

310. Leo Ruiz and Bernabe Salgado pick lemons for the Foothill Lemon Company, Corona, date unknown. **311.** At work in the Jameson packing house. Riverside, early 1940s. **312.** Angelo Anastasia with father, Joseph Anastasia Sr., in the family's fish market. Monterey, c. 1945. **313.** Victor Boido (second from right), owner of Boido Bakery, and his fleet of Harvest Bread trucks. South San Francisco, 1940s.

314

315

316

314. Cozy Café, Tyler Street, Monterey, 1941. **315.** Spanky of the Little Rascals, in a promotional photo for a meat market on Mission Street. San Francisco, 1930s.
316. Bill Potts (far right), butcher at the Taft Safeway store, c. 1930. **317.** Hamburger Johny's, San Francisco, 1933.

"Everybody loved Johny
because he would feed you
even when you couldn't pay."

Joseph Anmuth

318. Company workers at lunch in a packing shed. Selma, c. 1911. **319.** Cleaning up after Christmas dinner. Richmond, 1945. **320.** Kazuo Ito at the Obon Celebration in Anaheim: Squid Barbecue, c. 1993. **321.** Bagna cauda—hot garlic dip—in the Bugnattos' dining room. South San Francisco, 1940s.

320

321

> *"We knew the party was a success because the guests were falling over into the bushes as they left."*
>
> Ann Todd

322

323

324

325

326

327

328

322. The fiftieth wedding anniversary party of Robert and Florence McKever at El Caminito del Sur. Monterey, 1952. **323.** Barbecue on the Piazzoni Ranch. Carmel Valley, c. 1920. **324.** Poker game on Olive Avenue. South San Francisco, 1946. **325.** A "rotten Easter-egg hunt," two weeks after Easter. Whittier, 1998. **326.** Neddie Sloane's 82nd birthday party. Oakland, 1997. **327.** James Christian and Angelo Dillis at a backyard barbecue in South San Francisco, 1959. **328.** Toasting the bride and groom, Mary and Charles Coe. Berkeley, 1948.

329

330

332

333

334

337

338

331

335

336

339

340

341

342

343

341. Irene and Peter Chagaris in front of Pete's Coffee Shop. South San Francisco, 1948. **342.** Classmates. San Francisco, 1938. **343.** Brian Dedmon's birthday party. Whittier, 1954.

344

344. Clidell Wiggins and her friends camp out, c. 1956. Place unknown. **345.** Cassandra, Ann Elizabeth, and Nicholas Kashanski have a tea party. P.M.C. Frazier Park, 1998. **346.** Ron Sullivan's first birthday party. Marina district of San Francisco, 1931. **347.** The wedding of Vic and Jan (Slater) Lopez. Whittier, 1950.

345

346

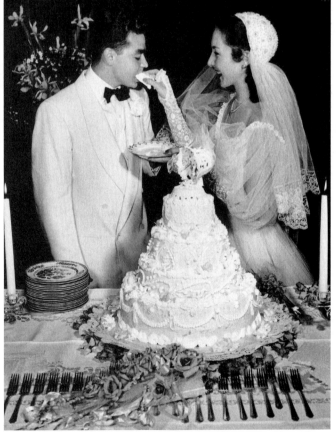

347

*"This is how I want
to be remembered."*

Charles F. Cuddy

A f t e r w o r d

From Shades of L.A. to Shades of California

Carolyn Kozo Cole and Kathy Kobayashi

The photographs in this book—as striking and varied as they are—are only the tip of the iceberg. They are simply the most visible part of Shades of California, a statewide photo-history project using images from family photo albums to document the daily lives of California's diverse communities and their historical, political, and cultural contributions.

What is remarkable about the Shades of California photos is that they show history from a perspective that is different from the usual view. Each participating community has searched its family albums for the photographs that were missing from the public record, and each has found images of people, places, and events rarely seen before by the public. Even more significantly, these photos show people and their communities from the inside, from their own point of view. These are not the images taken by photojournalists, television producers, or artists—outsiders, no matter how sympathetic. Instead, they are the photographs that people took of their own families and neighborhoods, the moments they chose to remember and save for themselves and for their children. Through the Shades project, people and their family albums, usually seen as passive subjects to be viewed and studied, have become active makers of their own history, defining what is important about their own lives.

To understand Shades of California, it is necessary first to step back and understand its origin, the Shades of L.A.

349

project. In 1990, researchers from the Southern California Library for Social Studies and Research came to the Los Angeles Public Library looking for images of Watts to use in a historical exhibit marking the twenty-fifth anniversary of the Watts riots. They weren't looking for images of rundown neighborhoods or burning buildings; they wanted to see the neighborhood before 1965, when it was a racially diverse but mostly African American neighborhood of neat streets, small, attractive homes, and thriving commerce. There was only one image in the Watts folder of the library's collection of 2.5 million photographs: the Pacific Electric

---

Carolyn Kozo Cole is curator of photographs at the Los Angeles Public Library and project director of Shades of L.A. Kathy Kobayashi is the historical consultant for Shades of L.A. and other projects with the photo collection.

railway station. In fact, few of Los Angeles's ethnic communities were represented in the collection.

As curator of the collection, I (Carolyn Kozo Cole) was determined to fill this gap in the public record and decided to look for people who had photos tucked away in their family albums or stored in their attics, and to copy those photos so that professional-quality prints and negatives could be available at the library for anyone interested in the history of Los Angeles. I turned for help to the Photo Friends of the L.A. Public Library, a nonprofit support group founded to help expand and promote the collection. Board member Ev McDonough presented the idea to Security Pacific National Bank, where he was executive vice-president, and secured funding for the pilot project in the African American community. Soon afterward, folklorist Amy Kitchener and historian Kathy Kobayashi were recruited to help coordinate the project.

With support from community leaders, educators, historians, and photographers, we tackled the problem of locating African American families with photographs from these early Los Angeles neighborhoods. In a massive community outreach effort—the key to the project, which was to be repeated each time the Shades model was taken to a new community—we contacted cultural centers, social organizations, churches, newspapers, radio and television stations, and local magazines. We culled names from borrowed mailing lists, sent out thousands of flyers, met with neighborhood activists, and enticed college professors and students enrolled in ethnic studies programs to help out.

Our next step was to host a series of "Photo Days" in African American communities. Our idea was that teams of volunteers, college interns, and library staff would sit with the donors at long tables and go through their albums, looking at the photographs, learning of their significance, selecting the images our photographers would copy— while the donors waited—and carefully recording the available details about each photo.

The biggest challenge was to persuade people to bring

their personal and prized possessions to a public place and share them with strangers. Some people felt vulnerable, even a little embarrassed to be sharing their photographs with the library, wondering whether the images they had long treasured could be of interest to people other than themselves and their own families. Most have come to believe in the project's mission and to feel strongly about the importance of making a contribution to the historical record.

On October 19, 1991, we kicked off our first Photo Day in the Vernon Branch Library at 42nd and Central Avenue, at the heart of what was once a swinging nightclub district, known in the 1940s as "the Stem." Today, the area is characterized by vacant lots, abandoned buildings, and a few modest storefronts. When our first donor, Mr. Toney, walked in, he was nearly overwhelmed by our pent-up enthusiasm. To our delight, the first images he pulled out of his grocery

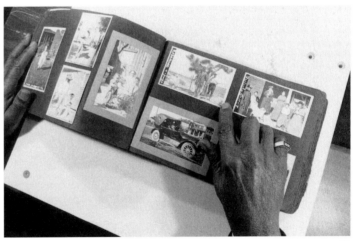

350

bags were of jazz clubs once located there on Central Avenue. They had been slipped into fancy, art-deco paper enclosures that identified the clubs with descriptions like "The Last Word—East Side's Smartest Sepia Night Club." By the end of the day, our two professional photographers, Bob Douglas and Coleman Grimmette, and their 6 x 7 medium-format cameras had copied over two hundred and fifty photographs—images that evoked stories, sometimes funny but always heartfelt, of black life in early Los Angeles.

This first Photo Day was a huge success, not only because of the history that we recovered from these albums, but because the process itself had the power to transform those sitting around the table—and this experience was repeated at each of the Photo Days to come. There we were—people of all ages and backgrounds—pencils in gloved hands, sitting side by side with families as they opened their albums and told the stories of their

351

lives in the images they gently placed before us. We looked and listened intently, writing down the stories behind the photos and finding out the details that future researchers might want to know. Tears and laughter comingled from table to table as the sharing went on; donors discovered themselves in other donors' albums, and long-lost memories were relived with such vividness that, for those moments, we became honorary members of their special lives. This experience connected us all deeply to the project and lured us back week after week to continue the search. With each of the different communities that came to our tables over the years, it was always a thrill to open the albums and listen as the stories began.

These feelings generated an overwhelming community response to the project. The phone in our office rang

continually, as self-appointed family historians answered the call to action. Shades of L.A. grew from that first Photo Day in the African American community into a seven-year project involving one thousand donors and volunteers, expanding into an ever broader view of Los Angeles. Folklorist Sojin Kim, photographer Judith Hopkins, and visual anthropologist Karin Stellwagen were brought in to coordinate the growing project. By the end, everyone was invited to the table—families from all of L.A.'s wide-ranging ethnic communities, as well as people who did not identify with any particular group.

Between 1991 and 1997, the Shades of L.A. project copied ten thousand photos from the family albums of communities in southern California, producing a permanent archive available to the public at the Los Angeles Public Library, as well as many exhibits, the book *Shades of L.A.: Pictures from Ethnic Family Albums* (Carolyn Kozo Cole and Kathy Kobayashi, New Press, 1996), a manual detailing project procedures, and thousands of images for the library's website, www.lapl.org.

Increasingly, the enthusiasm and sense of purpose sparked by Shades of L.A. caught the attention of people throughout the city and beyond—and we came to realize that Shades of L.A. was not just an effective local project, but could be used as a model for community history anywhere.

The idea for Shades of California first came from KCET-TV's Huell Howser, host of the *California's Gold* television show, who saw the remarkable success of the Shades of L.A. project and realized that communities all over the state of California needed to have their own Shades projects.

In 1997, we began to expand. First, with funding from the Durfee Foundation to the Library Foundation of Los Angeles, the Los Angeles Public Library took the Shades of L.A. model to libraries in San Francisco, Fresno, and San Bernardino Counties. Then, from 1997 to 1999, the California State Library supported the expansion of the model to still more libraries; with the help of Shades of L.A. staff hired as consultants, the California State Library issued a request for proposals to all the public libraries in the state, asking them to apply for funds to create their own local Shades projects. In that first year of Shades of California, 1997–98, the California State Library selected nine public libraries for funding; in the second year, fourteen public libraries were funded. Shades consultants helped local librarians and community coordinators to plan training workshops and Photo Days. The training workshops included a slide show on how to select the photographs to be copied, a manual detailing procedures, and a hands-on practice session. Each library's community chose its own focus for collecting. As expected, the excitement of the Photo Days was contagious.

The California State Library also provided technical assistance with the critical step of copying the images on Photo Days; after some trial and error, the State Library helped guarantee the quality of the photos by providing each Photo Day with two cameras, two copy stands, and one professional photographer experienced with the Shades project, and the local library provided one local professional photographer to gain expertise on the job.

By the end of the project, each library had copied several hundred valuable images and held a local Shades exhibit to publicly celebrate its new acquisitions, in addition to sending a set of prints to the California State Library's Shades of California archive; with major support from Library Services and Technology Act funds, the Shades project has created an archive of more than six thousand images collected by libraries across the state.

But the most important point is that each library has produced a set of negatives and prints for its local archive, to be used by future generations. Under the leadership of Dr. Kevin Starr, California State Librarian, Shades of California was designated by the California Sesquicentennial Commission as a legacy project, an important public resource not only for the commemoration that took place in the year 2000, but for many years to come.

352

Even now, in the twenty-first century, inspired by Shades of L.A. and Shades of California, communities in California continue to collect their photographic histories with local support and funding. And as people from other parts of the United States—and even other parts of the world—hear about the project, they are interested in replicating the Shades of L.A. model in their own communities. The possibilities are endless.

This excitement has spread well beyond the participants in the project. As soon as the first prints returned from the laboratory, we began to get calls requesting to use them. News of the project had spread rapidly by word of mouth and through the media: the *Los Angeles Times,* the *San Francisco Chronicle,* local newspapers and television stations, National Public Radio, and CNN all enthusiastically reported on the project. Thousands of people have used the photographs and been fascinated by them—from fourth graders studying California history to scholars at the Getty Research Institute, from independent documentary filmmakers to the creators of major Hollywood movies, from people working on their own family histories to playwrights and novelists. Others have seen the many Shades exhibits—

353

at libraries and community centers, historical societies and museums. One of the local projects, Shades of Monterey, has even made digitized images available for viewing in the waiting room of its community hospital.

What is the future of Shades of California? Our hope is that the spirit of the Shades project will continue to touch people and inspire them to see history in new ways. Those who want to use the Shades archives can contact the local libraries around the state (listed on the next page) to see the local photo collections, and even to order copies. The largest of these is the Shades of L.A. collection at the Los Angeles Public Library, and the California State Library also has copies of many of the photos. The heart of Shades of California, though, remains in the local photo collections, housed in their own communities. Each local collection—large or small—is significant and moving in its own way.

The spirit of Shades is not limited to the images already collected and archived. We hope that the simple idea behind Shades—copying people's photographs and recording their stories—will continue to spread. It can be replicated on a large scale—Shades of another state, Shades of America—but just as significantly, it can be done on a small scale—in a neighborhood, a school, a workplace, or a family reunion. In fact, any group of people who consider themselves a community can explore their own history in the spirit of Shades.

Finally, our hope is that all the individuals touched by Shades will look at their own family albums with fresh eyes and deeper appreciation. What has been done so far, then, is only a beginning.

List of Participating Libraries

1. Anaheim Public Library
2. Berkeley Public Library/South Branch
3. Corona Public Library
4. Escondido Public Library
5. Folsom Public Library
6. Fresno County Library, Fresno
7. Humboldt County Library
8. Kern County Library/Frazier Park Branch
9. Kern County Library/Taft Branch
10. Long Beach Public Library
11. Los Angeles Public Library
12. Madera County Library, Madera
13. Monterey Public Library
14. Oakland Public Library
15. Oxnard Public Library
16. Richmond Public Library
17. Riverside Public Library
18. San Bernardino County Library/Yucaipa Branch
19. San Bernardino Public Library
20. San Francisco Public Library
21. South San Francisco Public Library
22. Sutter County Library, Yuba City
23. Tulare County Library, Visalia
24. Watsonville Public Library
25. Whittier Public Library

Endnotes

1. SF-001-107 — San Francisco Public Library. Donor: Nettie Vance. Virginia Cook (Thomas) with her first Brownie camera. San Francisco, c. 1957. The donor took this picture of her sister Virginia and their friend Doris Howard just as Virginia was taking a picture of Nettie. Virginia, Nettie, and their brother Nelson had all received Brownies the previous Christmas.

2. SF-002-670 — San Francisco Public Library. Donor: Karen Hanning. Marie Mitchell's first communion. San Francisco, c. 1924. Marie's father gave her mother the cross that Marie wears in this picture when they became engaged. The couple were only sixteen and their families disapproved of their engagement, so he gave her the cross instead of a ring, as a secret pledge.

3. SF-002-236 — San Francisco Public Library. Donor: Lorraine Hazen. Vivian and Bernaby Guerrero (also pictured in 20) sitting in a rumble seat. Their father, John, is in front. San Francisco, c. 1930.

4. SSB-0-102 — San Bernardino Public Library. Donor: Mary Chartier. Dorothy Bright. San Bernardino, c. 1925. Dorothy owned a rare book store.

5. SSB-0-017 — San Bernardino Public Library. Donor: Ruth Mercer. John Mercer in his bedroom. San Bernardino, 1962. John and his father built and launched model rockets.

6. TA001-026 — Kern County Library / Taft Branch. Donor: Robert LeGar. Two girls and a motorcycle. Place and date unknown.

7. AN-001-824 — Anaheim Public Library. Donor: Daniel Albert. Pasqual (Pete) Daniel, cement contractor, poses for a formal portrait. Anaheim, c. 1901.

8. LB008-007 — Long Beach Public Library. Donor: Elvira Arvalo. Chuy Garcia and Minka Zorka. Long Beach, 1950s. The donor says Minka "always did like to dress up."

9. AN-001-125 — Anaheim Public Library. Donors: Rev. Carl and Miko Yoshimine. A group of friends, all members of the Japanese American Free Methodist Church in Anaheim, c. 1930. Left to right: Hiro Kitaoka, Paul Yano, Ben Watanabe, James Yano, Sam Yano. The donor says this is "either a funeral or a wedding, because they're all dressed up."

10. FOL-98-423 — Folsom Public Library. Donor: Marion C. Rader. The donor's grandfather, Joseph Washington Hill. Folsom, c. 1900.

11. SWAT-001-326 — Watsonville Public Library. Donor: Teresa Media. Maqui Arias. Watsonville, 1999. Teresa gave Maqui this photo she'd taken of her as a birthday present.

12. 98-001-012 — Escondido Public Library. Donor: Marian Peet. Rodolphus Peet, c. 1840. Place unknown.

13. LB008-010 — Long Beach Public Library. Donor: Elvira Arvalo. "The Three Little Sisters," Floriza, Mary, and Lolita Garcia, at Mary's wedding to Tommy Martinez. Long Beach, 1947. The girls made their own hats for Mary's wedding.

14. SB-000-002 — Berkeley Public Library / South Branch. Donor: Michiko Uchida. Berkeley girls in kimonos. Berkeley, c. 1929. This photo was taken at Lincoln School, now Malcolm X School. Left to right: Mary Sasajima, Helen Sasajima, Ruth Nishi, Kimiyo Kiuchi (now Irene Yoshimura), Michiko Fujii (now Uchida), Doris Kariya.

15. SSB-0-100 — San Bernardino Public Library. Donor: Ida Roberson. Cosmetology Group, Zeta Delta Chapter of the Alpha Chi Omega Sorority. San Bernardino, 1959. Left to right: Ida, Grayce McDonald, Ruth Saville, Lucille Williams, Jessie Lake, Alice Ballard, Savannah Williams, Esther Hargrove. The group was made up of cosmetologists and barbers and met in the members' homes.

16. SW5-038 — Whittier Public Library. Donor: Jan Lopez. Mary Love Slater. Berkeley, c. 1910–20. The photo shows the donor's mother, who was born in Berkeley in 1896.

17. AN-001-914 — Anaheim Public Library. Donor: Susan Liu. Katherine Liu celebrates graduation from Katella High School by posing with her brother David. Anaheim, c. 1996. The graduates were to take one traditional cap-and-gown photo and one photo with a prop. Katherine's brother David was home on leave, so she took him to the photo session as her "prop."

18. S-001-223 — Riverside Public Library. Donor: Rose Mayes. The high school prom. Rose Mayes and Aamos Ainsworth. Houston, Texas, 1961. The donor was seventeen and this was her first date. Rose (also pictured in 83), who had a strict mother, felt as though she "had just been set free."

19. FOL-98-130 — Folsom Public Library. Donor: Lois Briggs. Joan Briggs is installed as Worthy Advisor of the Rainbow Girls. Folsom, c. 1950s. Left to right: Raylene Davies, Joan Briggs, Charlene Greengalgh, Myrna Davies.

20. SF-002-244 — San Francisco Public Library. Donor: Lorraine Hazen. Bernaby Guerrero, daughter of John De Guerrero II, was the niece of Amalita De Guerrero (pictured in 22). Bernaby and her sister Vivian carried on the family tradition and became Spanish dancers.

21. S-012-242 — Los Angeles Public Library. Donors: Sam Balucas, Filipino American National Historical Society. It was usual in the Filipino community to take formal photographs of unmarried girls to show to potential suitors.

22. SF-002-238 — San Francisco Public Library. Donor: Lorraine Hazen. Amalita De Guerrero was the stage name of Carmelita De Guerrero. She and her sister Mary were widely known Spanish dancers in and around San Francisco at the turn of the twentieth century. Their mother was Mary Frances Berryessa, whose family came to California with de Anza. The donor has a postcard sent to Amalita from the king of Spain, professing his love for her and begging her to let him visit her. It ends: "I am no one of importance, being only the king of Spain."

23. PHO.99.Col.226-005 — Oakland Public Library. Donor: Ratha Watkins. Ratha did the hair and makeup on these models. Left to right: Coralie Collins, Ida Williams, Doris Anderson, Denise Dennis, and two unknown models who were managed by Billie Dunlap. According to Ratha, Slim Jenkins' was the top Oakland nightclub in the forties: "the only black place to go."

24. S98-001-044 — Oxnard Public Library. Donor: Anna Hidalgo Dennet.

25. FOL-98-425 — Folsom Public Library. Donor: Marion C. Rader. Charles E. Hill was the donor's great-uncle. She remembers him as a very sweet man and says of him: "Women just loved him; you can see it in his eyes."

26. S-001-234 — Riverside Public Library. Donor: Catherine Fitch.

27. SB-000-660 — Berkeley Public Library / South Branch. Donors: Ethel Tillman, Alexandra Jennings.

28. SW3-035 — Whittier Public Library. Donor: Georgenia Schmidt. Gladys and Rubie Whitaker, wearing outfits they made themselves. Whittier, 1934. The Whitaker sisters are the donor's aunts.

29. TCS1-097 — Tulare County Library. Donors: Tulare Historical Museum, Ling Joe family. Rosie Moey Yuen (Mrs. Yow Joe) and Daisy Joe. Tulare, 1914.

30. PHO.99.Col.221-006 — Oakland Public Library. Donor: Olivia Woods. Rosa and Olivia Woods. Oakland, c. 1988.

31. S1387 — Riverside Public Library. Donor: Lori Sisquoc. Blossom Sisquoc and Tanita Maciel. Riverside, 1997. Blossom and Tanita are Cahuilla and Ft. Sill Apache.

32. S1589 — Riverside Public Library. Donor: Doris Illes. Doris Illes and her mother at Grant Elementary School. Riverside, c. 1956. Doris's mother made the matching dresses they wear in the picture. Doris is an only child and still has breakfast with her mother every day. The Illes family came to the U.S. as Hungarian immigrants in 1954 after waiting for five years.

33. FOL-98-430 — Folsom Public Library. Donor: Marion C. Rader. Marion Caroline Saunders Hill with her niece, Flo Jones. Sacramento, early 1900s.

34. FOL-98-127 — Folsom Public Library. Donor: Lois Briggs. Lois and Joan Briggs wearing "sister" clothes made by their mother, Maggie Briggs. Folsom, 1950s.

35. PHO.99.Col.216-003 — Oakland Public Library. Donors: Mildred (O'Guinn) Leonard, Cathye Leonard. Liz O'Guinn and Mildred O'Guinn. Oakland, mid-1950s. The dent in the rear fender of the Dodge was put there by Mildred's future husband, Albert Leonard. (Mildred is also pictured in 126.)

36. SSB-0-320 — San Bernardino Public Library. Donor: August Santini. Twins Mary and Carol Pine (photographed in San Bernardino, 1944) also had twin girl cousins, the donor's daughters.

37. HU-000-263 — Humboldt County Library. Donor: Evelyn Waters. Evelyn Waters and her cousin Ruby Dunn from Pepperwood. Eureka, c. 1916. Evelyn was a talented singer who co-wrote a popular song in the 1920s, "A Dream Came True." Her father, "Swiftwater Bill" Waters, and Ruby's father, Jim Dunn, were saloon owners in Eureka and nearby Pepperwood.

38. FOL-98-117 — Folsom Public Library. Donor: Irene Harris. Irene Harris and Neva Cimaroli. Folsom, c. 1944.

39. SSF-001-137 — South San Francisco Public Library. Donor: Mary Metcalf.

40. TA001-611 — Kern County Library / Taft Branch. Donor: Catherine Edgecomb.

41. TCS1-220 — Tulare County Library. Donor: Jacque Lovelady. Daisy (Joe) Fung (also pictured in 29 and 243) says that everybody cried when she cut her hair to a fashionable bob in the 1920s. When she was a child the other children made fun of her given name, Gum, so she took a neighbor's suggestion and began to call herself Daisy. The first woman in town to fly in an airplane, she is now 105 years old.

42. SF-002-341 — San Francisco Public Library. Donor: Julie Collins. Left to right: Albert "Chubby" Nunan, holding his sister Marianne Patricia "Patsy" Nunan, Anita Juliette "Reedy" Nunan holding baby Donald, (back) Robert "Bobby" Nunan, (front) Dorothy Hean. The photo was taken to show off Reedy's new "Irene Castle" bob.

43. SF-002-703 — San Francisco Public Library. Donor: Ron Sullivan. This photo of Mary (also pictured in 346) was taken shortly before her marriage.

44. SF-002-362 — San Francisco Public Library. Donor: Julie Collins. Julie believes that this party was a send-off for one of the Fontana brothers as he left to fight in WWII. Left to right: Mrs. Domenic (Dorothy Jean Nunan) Fontana, Mrs. Pasquale (Elsie Cavagnaro) Fontana, Mrs. Albert (Inez Fontana) Leonardini, and Florence Fontana (later Mrs. Dino Queirolo).

45. SF-001-121 — San Francisco Public Library. Donor: Oscar Bertram.

46. SF-002-636 — San Francisco Public Library. Donor: Mary Kerrigan.

47. LB008-354 — Long Beach Public Library. Donor: Susie Stanford. The Pike was an amusement park on the beach in Long Beach from 1902 to the 1980s.

48. HU-000-229 — Humboldt County Library. Donor: Jeanne Johnson Nash. Madeline graduated from Humboldt State University in 1917 and taught for two years. One year after meeting her husband she contracted tuberculosis. She had two children before her death in 1926.

49. KC-001-217 — Kern County Library / Frazier Park Branch. Donor: Nancy Kashanski. Nancy took this photograph of her daughter (also pictured in 345).

50. SW1-022 — Whittier Public Library. Donor: Marie A. Kaneko. Manuel, Ignacio's father, was killed shortly after the photo was taken, stabbed by one of his shepherds, whom he had accused of stealing sheep.

51. PHO.99.Col.237-001 — Oakland Public Library. Donor: Audrey Robinson. Thelma Gibson, born in 1903, became a nurse. Audrey, born in 1915, became a teacher. Lois (also pictured in 298) was born in 1906. She became a podiatrist.

52. PHO.99.Col.201-003 — Oakland Public Library. Donor: Kathy Sloane. Kathy called this photo "Ask Yo' Mama" after the Langston Hughes poem "Ask Your Mama." The three girls, dressed in their mothers' clothes, are on their way to a birthday party. Najuma's mother, Barbara Christian, was the first tenured African American woman at UC Berkeley. Nalungo was a neighbor and Ayisha is the donor's daughter.

53. LB008-271 — Long Beach Public Library. Donor: Wang L. Xiong. Gorlian's father, Wang Xiong, makes these traditional musical instruments, called gheng or qeej.

54. SW2-020 — Whittier Public Library. Donor: Glenn Chambers.

55. SW4-020 — Whittier Public Library. Donor: Mary Karasawa. Left to right: Karen (also pictured in 182), Patty, Nancy, and John Karasawa.

56. SSB-0-518 — San Bernardino Public Library. Donor: Manuel Gomez.

57. SSF-001-156 — South San Francisco Public Library. Donor: Mary Giusti.

58. SF-002-323 — San Francisco Public Library. Donor: Caroline Mota.

59. SF-002-319 — San Francisco Public Library. Donor: Caroline Mota.

60. SW2-015 — Whittier Public Library. Donor: Julie Padilla. The Abajian children, left to right: Samuel (who died in the Russian revolution), Aramise, Badvagan (who died soon after coming to the U.S.), and Baitzar. The family came on the Greek ship *Themistocles*.

61. SW1-053 — Whittier Public Library. Donor: Ann Ybarra. The O'Donnell boys' mother was from San Francisco, where shorts were considered the proper attire for boys, but the boys grew up in San Luis Obispo, where corduroys were more usual. The O'Donnell boys suffered some on account of their shorts.

62. LB008-004 — Long Beach Public Library. Donor: Elvira (Garcia) Arvalo. Elvira's mother made the dress and headband of maroon fabric. Elvira's babysitter gave her the doll and took the picture.

63. LB008-118 — Long Beach Public Library. Donor: Connie Williams.

64. S-001-040 — San Francisco Public Library. Donor: Lorraine Dillon. Left to right: Christabel Thompson, Catherine Lucey, Lorraine Spottiswood (now Dillon), Margaret Pettee, Marian Neeper. The donor still has her doll and, except for Marian Neper, is still in touch with the others in the picture.

65. S-008-072 — Los Angeles Public Library. Donor: Luther Eskijian. Left to right: Helen Barsumian, Luther Eskijian, Josephine Barsumian, Harry Ekmekjian, John Eskijian, Seth Ekmekjian.

66. TA001-232 — Kern County Library / Taft Branch. Donor: Karen Mitchell. Walter Schmidt, a local photographer, took the photo.

67. S-01-309 — Sutter County Library. Donor: Sharon Shimizu. The photo shows the donor and her sister.

68. SB000-149 — San Bernardino County Library / Yucaipa Branch. Donor: Thelma Miller. The donor owned the Yucaipa Theater from 1947 to 1952. Thelma says, "The kids used to come on horseback. They tied their horses behind the theater." Adults paid fifty cents to see a movie; kids paid a dime.

69. TCS1-299 — Tulare County Library. Donor: Ora Fong. The donor's brother, Harry Gong, is third from the right (standing).

70. S-001-667 — Riverside Public Library. Donor: Rose Medina. This is Rose's kindergarten photo. Her mother was upset because she didn't know it was photo day and didn't have a chance to dress her up.

71. PHO.99.Col.201-049 — Oakland Public Library. Donor: Kathy Sloane.

72. TA001-135 — Kern County Library / Taft Branch. Donor: Pat Soles.

73. RCH-351 — Richmond Public Library. Donor: Kathleen Rupley. Kathleen thinks this was taken on the first day of school, shortly after a summer trip to Disneyland; the clue is the Disneyland lunch box.

74. PHO.99.Col.201-032 — Oakland Public Library. Donor: Kathy Sloane. Camp Read-A-Lot was a reading program held in schools all over Oakland and sponsored by the mayor's office.

75. TA001-115 — Kern County Library / Taft Branch. Donor: Pete Gianopulos. Mary Hall later became a teacher in Taft. She taught there until she retired.

76. SF-002-118 — San Francisco Public Library. Donor: Tina Townsend. Tina took the picture of this group of friends near graduation. The boy in front, Joe Brotnik, became a San Francisco policeman. He was killed on duty. The couple behind him, Tom Combis and Eleanor Jestings, later married. The group are all still friends.

77. S98-001-013 — Oxnard Public Library. Donor: Jeff Maulhardt.

78. 98-001-421 — Escondido Public Library. Donor: Marilyn Shriver.

79. SSB-0-233 — San Bernardino Public Library. Donor: Judith Valles.

80. SSB-0-358 — San Bernardino Public Library. Donor: Shelley Silver. Aaron's store was in the downtown Hispanic area of San Bernardino. Aaron's mother owned a restaurant / general store near El Paso, Texas, which was where Aaron had learned Spanish. Nicknamed "the Angel" by Hispanics because he treated them with respect, he had a one-dollar-down credit policy. The store is still family-owned.

81. LB008-452 — Long Beach Public Library. Donor: Theresa Steiner. A. H. and Dean Wille opened the Wet Wash Laundry in 1913. In 1917 they held a contest to rename it, and Mrs. C. E. Newell won ten dollars for the winning entry: Long Beach Steam Laundry.

82. FOL-98-226 — Folsom Public Library. Donor: Dee Rumsey.

83. S-001-214 — Riverside Public Library. Donor: Rose Mayes. While in college, Rose walked into a record store which was for sale, offered the owner $500, and worked off the rest of the cost, later expanding to three stores.

84. HU-000-109 — Humboldt County Library. Donor: Bruno Ravelli. Tony Ravelli learned the shoe repair trade in Italy. He started his young son, Bruno, in the family business, telling him, "You won't make no money playing football." Since Bruno was only six or seven at the time, his father kept a large block of wood in the store to enable him to reach the equipment.

85. SSF-001-229 — South San Francisco Public Library. Donor: Bill Helfrich.

86. SSB-0-043 — San Bernardino Public Library. Donor: Rachel (Mendoza) Clark.

87. S-010-232 — Los Angeles Public Library. Donors: A. Peter Kezirian Jr., Marilyn Tevriz Kezirian.

88. 98-02-024 — Fresno County Library. Donor: Diana Bell.

89. HU-001-401 — Humboldt County Library. Donor: James Kim Bauriedel, M.D.

90. HU-000-064 — Humboldt County Library. Donors: Barbara McNeely, Arleen Young. Three mail carriers. Eureka, c. 1897.

91. PHO.99.Col.201-007 — Oakland Public Library. Donor: Kathy Sloane. Dr. Melanie Turvelon, examining a child with Down's syndrome as the child's mother looks on. Oakland, 1990s. The photo was taken at Children's Hospital outpatient clinic.

92. SW5-012 — Whittier Public Library. Donor: Regina Phelan. John J. Phelan is shown hauling telephone poles to Whittier in horse-drawn wagons. Whittier, 1910. Mr. Phelan was later hit by a car, thrown from the wagon, and crippled.

93. PHO.99.Col.217-003 — Oakland Public Library. Donor: Betty Edwards. James J. Bryant, Pullman porter, and his wife, Florence, on his retirement from the railroad. Oakland, 1950s. In 1954, Florence Bryant was Oakland's first Mother of the Year.

94. TA001-106 — Kern County Library / Taft Branch. Donor: Marge Tiffany. Installing the new computer lab at Taft College. Taft, 1984. Left to right: Dr. Don Greene, Dr. David Cethrun, Kirk Brettschneider, Bill Baker, Dr. John Tuft.

95. RCH-043 — Richmond Public Library. Donors: Linda and Elsie Olvera. Joe Olvera (left), in front of a police patrol wagon. Richmond, 1947. Mr. Olvera was a Richmond policeman from 1945 to 1957.

96. MTY-6404 — Monterey Public Library. Donors: Carolyn and Gary Carlsen. Employees of First National Bank, Alvarado Street. Monterey, c. 1959.

97. TA001-607 — Kern County Library / Taft Branch. Donor: Gary Graupman. Jim Norris and two unknown oil workers, working for Western Well. Taft, c. 1977.

98. RCH-410 — Richmond Public Library. Donor: Nettie Lopez. Carolyn Lopez Ross working at her brother's business, Creative Signs. Richmond, late 1970s.

99. 98-001-207 — Escondido Public Library. Donor: Alice Webb Inga. The Webb Brothers' Massey-Harris tractor display at the Del Mar Fair in 1945. The donor's father owned a tractor store. This photo shows the yearly tractor show.

100. TA001-219 — Kern County Library / Taft Branch. Donor: Don Henshaw. The Belgium Oil Company crew. Fellows, 1902.

101. SW5-004 — Whittier Public Library. Donors: Paul and Annie Zolnekoff. The men are pouring a concrete foundation for a den addition to Annie and Paul Zolnekoff's house on McGee Street in Whittier.

102. SF-002-248 — San Francisco Public Library. Donor: Lorraine Hazen. Like her sister Carmelita, Mary performed as a Spanish dancer.

103. AN-001-189 — Anaheim Public Library. Donor: Harry Kitahata. Harry, an elderly man, discovered when he got to the library that he'd forgotten his photos. It was so important to him to participate in the project that he returned home, got them, and drove back to the library. In all, he drove eighty miles through heavy L.A. traffic that day.

104. COR-98-SH051 — Corona Public Library. Donor: Ray Aparicio. A freeway now runs through the land on which the house stood.

105. COR-98-SHO38 — Corona Public Library. Donor: Dolores Ortiz Salgado.

106. SF-002-634 — San Francisco Public Library. Donor: Mary Kerrigan. George was a big baseball fan. The hat he's wearing in this picture covers bald patches from one of his frequent hair-pulling fights with his friend Dennis Finnegan. (George and Arthur are also pictured in 264.)

107. HU-001-037 — Humboldt County Library. Donor: Cheryl Franchesci.

108. SW5-033 — Whittier Public Library. Donor: Jan Lopez. Left to right: Joyce Ashby, Dorothy Francis, Carol Beatty, Mary Acker, and the donor (also pictured in 347). The school went to the finals in basketball the year this photo was taken. The pom-poms, made of crepe paper, were ritually burned each week after the game. One time Jan got too close to the fire and singed her eyebrows.

109. TA001-215 — Kern County Library / Taft Branch. Donor: Patricia Soles. Wesley's older brother bought this uniform for him.

110. PHO.99.Col.220-005 — Oakland Public Library. Donor: Michael Hammock. The game was the semifinals of the Oakland Little League Young American Baseball Champs. Michael's team won the championship.

111. TA001-223a — Kern County Library / Taft Branch. Donor: Dorothy Henshaw. Dorothy founded the Taft School of Sport Parachuting in 1961 with her husband, Art, but he would never let her make a jump. He was apparently a man of iron. Though sympathetic to her desire to skydive, none of the staff members would take her up; they were afraid of losing their jobs. On the way home from Art's funeral (on Dorothy's 66th birthday), some of the staff insisted that Dorothy stop at the airstrip. They told her they wanted to take her up to make her first jump. She thought to herself, "If I don't do it now, then forget it!" and let them strap on the parachute rig. The photo depicts her first dive.

112. LB008-248 — Long Beach Public Library. Donor: Tom Flores. This team was made up of cable splicers working for GTE (now Verizon). Left to right: John Spaulding, Tom Flores, Henry Romero, Cecelia Crisantes, John Olson, and Ron Baldwin. Though some are retired and some have moved to other areas, they all still keep in touch.

113. TA001-444 — Kern County Library / Taft Branch. Donor: Janet Meachem Lee. Mamma Jane is in center; Minnie Meachem, the donor's grandmother, is on her right.

114. MTY-7025 — Monterey Public Library. Donor: Sachi Oka. Back row, left to right: Aiko (last name unknown), Kimiko Higishi, Sachi Higuchi Oka, Nobuko Higashi Takigawa. Front row, left to right: Sako Gota, Yoshi Higuchi, the sensei (teacher, name unknown), Aiko Hattori, Yoshiko Hattori Miyamoto. Kendo is a Japanese martial art that evolved from sword fighting.

115. S-012-841 — Los Angeles Public Library. Donor: Jim Dimitriou. The Greek atheletes in the photo toured the country in the twenties.

116. COR-98-SH020 — Corona Public Library. Donor: Dolores Ortiz Salgado.

117. SWAT-001-106 — Watsonville Public Library. Donor: Gary Soper. Harold Soper, born in 1893, drove a horse and wagon for Wells Fargo and later worked as an engineer for the Southern Pacific Railroad. He retired in 1970. The dog Rascal was so called because he pulled down clotheslines and knocked over flowerpots.

118. S-01-504 — Sutter County Library. Donor: Leigh Graves. Percy Graves was a grain farmer.

119. FOL-98-604 — Folsom Public Library. Donor: Jim Davies.

120. PHO.99.Col.227-004 — Oakland Public Library. Donor: Carnella Butler. Kennidi models for Mervyn's department stores.

121. S-01-166 — Sutter County Library. Donor: Katy Lim. Roy Rogers used to visit Sutter County often because he stabled his horse, Trigger, there in the summer. Katy Lim remembers evening sing-alongs at which everyone was welcome. Says Ms. Lim: "Roy didn't care who you were," referring to his friendliness.

122. S-01-418 — Sutter County Library. Donor: John Brownlee.

123. LB008-011 — Long Beach Public Library. Donor: Vera Arvalo.

124. MTY-6834 — Monterey Public Library. Donor: Meg Morris.

125. SSB-0-235 — San Bernardino Public Library. Donor: Bonnie Hinds. This was a publicity picture taken at the California Hotel for KFXM. Bonnie Hinds and Evalyn Erickson formed a country-western singing group among the children of their neighborhood, which performed on KFXM. First row, left to right: Norman Newberry, John Christenson, Buddy Erickson, Paul Christenson. Second row: Joe Mueller, Derryll (last name unknown), Tommy Hysong, Josie Mueller, Norma Christenson. Third row: Eleanor St. John, Bonnie Hinds, Evalyn Erickson, (unidentified woman), and the show's host, "Uncle Berry."

126. PHO.99.Col.216-008 — Oakland Public Library. Donors: Mildred (O'Guinn) Leonard, Cathye Leonard. Mildred O'Guinn (also pictured in 35) on a pony owned by an itinerant photographer who would take pictures of children and sell the photos to their parents.

127. MTY-6646 — Monterey Public Library. Donor: Marge Turnbull. Abe McFadden was a cattle rancher who ran his place, Garza's Ranch, as a kind of resort.

128. SWAT-001-124 — Watsonville Public Library. Donor: Gary Soper. Ernie Furrer, second from right, was married to the donor's aunt Tessie. The story goes that Ernie was a city boy and his wife wouldn't go near the horses.

129. S-012-378 — Los Angeles Public Library. Donor: Joe Palicte.

130. PHO.99.Col.211-003 — Oakland Public Library. Donor: Raymond Holbert. The man sitting in the car is Kaiser Henderson. The photo was taken at Mosswood Park, where the Van Dykes met each month for their caravan to Santa Cruz. They organized hayrides, dances, picnics, and trips. The group members wore blazers and sweaters with the letters "VD" in gold. "That caused us some problems," says Raymond.

131. SSB-0-404 — San Bernardino Public Library. Donor: Danny Flores. The car was painted by Fred Payan. Danny says, "Everybody in town knows my car."

132. TA001-129 — Kern County Library / Taft Branch. Donor: Patricia Soles.

133. SB-000-626 — Berkeley Public Library / South Branch. Donor: Karen Hata. Bill Hata in front of the family Model T on Stuart Street. Berkeley, c. 1925.

134. S-01-437 — Sutter County Library. Donor: Judy Hale. The photo shows C. E. and Alice Reische with their first Buick. Kilgore Road, Meridian, 1930. Alice was stunned when C. E. brought home the Buick, because he'd always bought used cars before.

135. S-01-339 — Sutter County Library. Donor: Don Burtis. The Burtis family on a road trip. Lodi, 1958. Left to right: Colleen, Kenneth, Eileen, Beryl, and Don Burtis.

136. S98-003-009 — Oxnard Public Library. Donor: Carolyn Koontz Vaughn. Robert and Emma Lane with their children and grandchildren. Oxnard, c. 1947.

137. TA001-005 — Kern County Library / Taft Branch. Donor: Randy Miller. Jim White and his wife, Faye, pose in front of their Model T Ford with their children Vane and Ila and a sister-in-law, Ruth Baldwin, on a family trip to Long Beach, c. 1930.

138. LB008-218 — Long Beach Public Library. Donor: Linda Tovar Garza. The Tovar children. Bellflower, late 1950s. The children are (left to right): Donald, Eddie, Paul, and Linda Tovar.

139. SW1-046 — Whittier Public Library. Donor: Ann Ybarra.

Gloria and Anthony Ybarra on vacation. Ensenada, Mexico, 1949.

140. MTY-6015 — Monterey Public Library. Donor: Margaret (Branson) Wenzel. Children with an Art Cleaners truck on Watson Street, Monterey, c. 1940. Many Italians lived in this neighborhood, known as "Spaghetti Hill." Middle girl: Maggie Branson.

141. RCH-340 — Richmond Public Library. Donor: Janette Russey. Richmond, 1969. The donor inherited Grandma's 1966 Volkswagen beetle. Janette loved this car. She met her future husband when, during one of the aging car's frequent breakdowns, he helped her push it. She drove the car until the day the gearshift lever came off in her hand and her father coolly observed that it might be time to buy a new car.

142. RCH-019 — Richmond Public Library. Donor: Shahrzad Khorsandi. The donor (left) and her friend Nafisa Shams with Shahrzad's sixteenth birthday present—her first car. Pinole, 1985. Shahrzad once fit ten people into the car. She almost got her first ticket, for speeding, on the day she left for college. The policeman asked her why she was crying. When she told him she was sad at leaving her home and friends, he let her go without a citation.

143. KC-001-523 — Kern County Library / Frazier Park Branch. Donor: Carol Darling. Frances Tubbs (second from left) and some friends. Frazier Park, 1930s.

144. LB008-362 — Long Beach Public Library. Donor: Susie Stanford. Lisa Castillo on her bike in front of her home. Long Beach, 1974.

145. TCS1-217 — Tulare County Library. Donor: Larry Ishimoto. Left to right: George Tsuneta, Asako Tsuneta with her daughter Julia, Itsuno Tsuneta, Shizuge Tsuneta (now Hada), Kimiye Tsuneta (now Tanizaki), and Frank Tsuneta.

146. MTY-6828 — Monterey Public Library. Donor: Ann Quattlebaum. Ben worked for the city of Monterey. His daughter Ann says that her late father was usually all business.

147. FOL-98-704 — Folsom Public Library. Donor: Claire and Lindsay Taylor.

148. PHO.99.Col.237-005 — Oakland Public Library. Donor: Audrey Robinson.

149. SSB-0-311 — San Bernardino Public Library. Donor: Annette Overstreet.

150. S-001-657 — Riverside Public Library. Donor: Rose Medina.

151. SSB-0-225 — San Bernardino Public Library. Donor: Sue Payne. Sue's friend Bill Becker (pictured) rescued his neighbors' pets during the Panorama fire. The Payne house was saved by neighborhood kids who stayed behind and fought the fire with garden hoses. The fire came so close that the lawn burned—as did a fire truck parked in front.

152. SWAT-001-322 — Watsonville Public Library. Donor: Gabriela Hernandez. As the decoration of her mother's living room testifies, Ms. Hernandez grew up in a devout Catholic family. She now takes her own children to the church she attended every Sunday as a child. She still owns the TV shown in the picture.

153. SWAT-001-166 — Watsonville Public Library. Donor: Peggy Burdick.

154. S-001-659 — Riverside Public Library. Donor: Rose Medina. Rose says of her mother: "Mom won't behave. We can't take her anyplace."

155. AN-001-629 — Anaheim Public Library. Donor: Lupe E. Reyes.

156. SB-000-470 — Berkeley Public Library / South Branch. Donor: Mary Trahan.

157. TA001-133 — Kern County Library / Taft Branch. Donor: Patricia Soles. Left to right: Richard, Vicky, and Patricia Stewart. The cowboy outfits were a Christmas gift from the children's mother, who made new costumes every Christmas. On the left were the children's brand-new Christmas bicycles— their very first.

158. AN-001-625 — Anaheim Public Library. Donor: Lupe E. Reyes. RoseMarie expected a gift on the occasion of her first communion. Taken by surprise, her grandparents gave her a pineapple which they had on hand. RoseMarie was happy with her "special gift."

159. S-008-361 — Los Angeles Public Library. Donor: Parviz Gharib-Afshar. It's a Persian tradition to jump over the fire on the last day of the Persian year so that the warmth of the fire will stay with the jumper.

160. 98-001-049 — Escondido Public Library. Donor: Eloise Paredes. Queen Eloise Lozano (the picture's donor), center, is flanked by attendants Eleanor Valdez and Lupe Contreras. Eloise said that her picture was put up on posters all over town, so people started greeting her in the street. She was mystified until she saw the posters, some of which had mustaches drawn on them.

161. PHO.99.Col.235-001 — Oakland Public Library. Donor: Josephine Lee. Left to right: Acie Lee, Josephine Lee, Raymond Ramey, Mary Ramey, James Shepard, Jeanne Shepard.

162. S1442–Riverside Public Library. Donor: Dr. Shamel Abd-Allah. The celebration of Eid-al-Fitr is always joyous. Of the fasting of Ramadan, Dr. Abd-Allah says, "Every day of fasting protects you from hell."

163. SSB-0-363 — San Bernardino Public Library. Donor: Masako Hirata. Tomiko, son of Kumajiro and Same, was one and a half years old when he died. The young girl in the white dress is Helen Hirata.

164. AN-001-652 — Anaheim Public Library. Donor: Vera Castro. The baby died a month after he was born; his father, Tiofolo, died a year later of tuberculosis.

165. SW1-026 — Whittier Public Library. Donor: Marie A. Kaneko.

166. S98-001-053 — Oxnard Public Library. Donor: Anna Hidalgo Dennett.

167. SSF-001-200 — South San Francisco Public Library. Donor: Marc Teglia.

168. HU-000-238 — Humboldt County Library. Donor: Ben Chin. Ben was drafted into the army at the age of 22. The only Chinese American in a company of 150, he fought for three years in WWII. After being honorably discharged, he opened a restaurant in Eureka. For the first three weeks there was a barrage of threatening and obscene racist phone calls. After this stopped, he found his customers to be courteous. Ben says, "They told me how courageous I was." He credits the popularity of his wife, Mary, with much of the restaurant's success.

169. S1804 — Riverside Public Library. Donor: Tina Zdilor. The donor was amazed that her mother, Nadaline, worked in Flight Operations in the Women's Marine Corps during WWII. F.O. was the forerunner of modern air traffic control. Tina knows her mother only as a "1950s stay-at-home mom who didn't even drive."

170. LB008-075 — Long Beach Public Library. Donor: Stan Poe. After his stint as a soldier, Glenn Baker married and became a farmer in the early 1900s. At one point he made a deal with the neighboring Bixby family to buy one of their cows. The Bakers drove their car over to the Bixbys', intending to tether the cow to the car and drive slowly home. In the meantime, the cow had calved. The calf was too young to walk the distance, so they loaded it into the back of the car. The family diaries make no further mention of the transaction except to note, three days later: "Glenn finally cleaned out the back of the car."

171. PHO.99.Col.213-028 — Oakland Public Library. Donor: Carl C. Mack. Mr. Mack, the man at the lower right, was district executive for Boy Scouts of America in the 1950s.

172. AN-001-839 — Anaheim Public Library. Donor: Frank and Mary Hirahara. Though cameras were not allowed in WWII Japanese American internment camps, some internees smuggled them in; others were able to order them from the Montgomery Ward catalog at the camp store. Bud Arayama was head of the camera club. George Hirahara, second from left, cut a hole in the floor of his family's quarters to make a darkroom below. Among the photographic equipment he hid was an enlarger ordered through the camp store.

173. LB008-334 — Long Beach Public Library. Donor: United Cambodian Community.

174. SWAT-001-091 — Watsonville Public Library. Donor: Oscar Rios. Left to right: Alejandro Chavez, Beto Luevano, Andres (last name unknown), Carlos Lanbavary, Eddie Cordova, Oscar Rios, Daniel, and Tony (last names unknown).

175. SSF-001-252 — South San Francisco Public Library. Donor: Eleanore Fourie.

176. HU-000-095 — Humboldt County Library. Donor: Noel Harris. This was a roving picket line. The workers went on strike in support of an Oregon strike against M & M Lumber.

177. SW4-044 — Whittier Public Library. Donor: Armando Baeza. Left to right: Richard Peña, Leticia Peña Rodella, Lisa Peña, Anna Maria Baeza, Alice S. Baeza, Fernando Peña, Raul Baeza, Frank Hernandez, Jesus N. Hernandez.

178. TCS1-467 — Tulare County Library. Donor: Gayle Kajioka.

179. S-01-438 — Sutter County Library. Donor: Judy Hale.

180. PHO.99.Col.201-004 — Oakland Public Library. Donor: Kathy Sloane. This photo of the Richardsons was taken on the occasion of their winning the Koshland Civic Unity Award from the San Francisco Foundation, which seeks to honor unsung community heroes. Kathy says this was "a wonderful day of stories" at Marcus Books.

181. S-007-664 — Los Angeles Public Library. Donor: Silva Dakessian. Left to right: Vache Madenlian, Bedros Kumashian, Simon Gharidian. Rear group: Shavarsh Balbalian, Sarkis Dakessian, Jack Deukmejian, Makrouhi Dakessian, Arevalous Dakessian, Takouhi Cazian. Front group: Arthur Dakessian, Kevork Dakessian, Raffi Dakessian, unknown. The family, except for Kevork, immigrated to California from Jordan. Kevork visits every year, and on this occasion family members were putting on a skit in his honor.

182. SW4-017 — Whittier Public Library. Donor: Mary Karasawa. Left to right: Sandy Siler, Doreen Gates, Karen Karasawa.

183. RCH-431 — Richmond Public Library. Donor: Nancy Pothyphom.

184. TCS1-320 — Tulare County Library. Donor: Gayle Kajioka. The donor's grandfather Yoshikazu Morioka, a citrus farmer, is at the top of the pyramid. He is standing on the shoulders of Tom Sakamoto and a friend named Konya, and they are on the shoulders of an unknown man, a friend named Yoshimura, and Satsuyo G. Sakamoto.

185. SB-000-592 — Berkeley Public Library / South Branch. Donor: Sally Levinson.

186. SB-000-310 — Berkeley Public Library / South Branch. Donor: Martha Ann Hilliard. Every Thursday was "Dad's day out."

187. KC-001-482 — Kern County Library / Frazier Park Branch. Donor: Karen Dustman. Sheriff Tibbet was later killed in a famous shootout with the outlaw Jim Kinney. His son Laurence Tibbet later became a well-known opera singer.

188. 98-01-055 — Madera County Library. Donor: Lupe Garcia.

189. S-01-307 — Sutter County Library. Donor: Sharon Shimizu. The fishermen are the donor's mother's cousin and his father.

190. SWAT-001-007 — Watsonville Public Library. Donor: Serafina Ramirez. What looks like a bar is actually a Wild West photo set; the Santa Cruz Beach Boardwalk had a photo concession in which people could have pictures taken in either a mock jail or barroom.

191. 98-001-324 — Escondido Public Library. Donor: James Bulen Jr.

192. RCH-317 — Richmond Public Library. Donor: Beatrix Watson. The mini-float is built around Judy's wheelchair. Judy and her mother, Beatrix, have made a hobby of producing costumes for people from all over the country during Carnaval. Asked where she got the inspiration for this work, Beatrix replied, "It comes from the heart, darlin'. It comes from the heart."

193. TA001-406 — Kern County Library / Taft Branch. Donor: Esther Livingston.

194. COR-98-SH249 — Corona Public Library. Donor: Frances Martinez.

195. 98-04-013A — Madera County Library. Donor: Shirley Ann Richardson.

196. TA001-421 — Kern County Library / Taft Branch. Donor: Pete Gianopulos.

197. TA001-417 — Kern County Library / Taft Branch. Donor: Pete Gianopulos. Oildorado Days, started in 1930 and held every five years (except during WWII) celebrates the Taft area's longtime oil industry. People dress in the Gay Nineties style of the early oil days and there are contests of skill among the oil workers.

198. 98-01-0055 — Fresno County Library. Donor: Lillie Lew.

199. 98-01-032 — Madera County Library. Donor: Verna Jones.

200. TA001-601 — Kern County Library / Taft Branch. Donor: Glenn Dolder Black. Vic Borrecco owned a shoe store. Ed Bigham, who worked for Sparkle Cleaners, was a member of the chamber of commerce. The photo was taken to promote Taft businesses.

201. KC-001-247 — Kern County Library / Frazier Park Branch. Donor: Gloria Cuddy.

202. RCH-347 — Richmond Public Library. Donor: Kathleen Rupley. Left to right: Bob Rupley, Jim Crough, Patricia Rupley. "Poker was very important to my family," says Kathleen.

203. LB008-130 — Long Beach Public Library. Donor: Debbie Gale.

204. SF-002-259 — San Francisco Public Library. Donors: Ted and Inez Scourkes. The families all piled into the truck to go on their picnic. Front row: Robert Draggis, Gregory Draggis, Gregory Pantages, Georgia Pantages, Nickie Pantages, Georgia Draggis, Helen Pantages, Theodore Scourkes, Melpomane (Mae) Scourkes, Gus Scourkes. Middle row: Peter Draggis, Nick Draggis, Theodora Draggis, Georgia Panayakis, Vula Pantages, Aunt Draggis, Evyenia Pantelakis Scourkes, George Pantelakis. Back row: Peter Pantages, George Pantages, John Pantages.

205. S-001-614 — Riverside Public Library. Donor: Rose Medina. Left to right: Louie, Barbara (also pictured in 154), Rose, Gilbert, Mary Lou, Jamie, Christina, and Gabriel Lopez. The family went to Knott's Berry Farm frequently. Admission was free in those days and "it was the only place cheap enough to take all those kids," according to Rose (Lopez) Medina.

206. LB008-451 — Long Beach Public Library. Donor: Theresa Steiner. Contrary to appearances, the men are not part of a swim team. Most of them arrived from Spearfish, South Dakota, for a visit to Long Beach without swimwear; the swimsuits were all bought at the same time. Dean Wille, far right, is Alva Haworth Wille's son and the donor's father.

207. S-01-421 — Sutter County Library. Donor: John Brownlee. The "swimming hole" was an irrigation canal.

208. COR-98-SH003 — Corona Public Library. Donor: Suzanne MacConnell.

209. SF-002-246 — San Francisco Public Library. Donor: Lorraine Hazen.

210. MTY-6627 — Monterey Public Library. Donor: Elizabeth Leeper. Left to right: Elizabeth Leeper, Nan Shepard, Col. Millard Shepard, Dana Godbe. The Shepards were Liz Leeper's aunt and uncle. They came expressly to sit in the new hot tub. Unexpectedly, they brought swimsuits, "so we all had to wear suits too."

211. SWAT-001-444 — Watsonville Public Library. Donor: Harold Hyde. The Watsonville Methodist Church celebrated Decoration Day (now Memorial Day) with a picnic at the beach.

212. S1445 — Riverside Public Library. Donor: Marillyn and Warren Shine. Helen was worried about a tear in the seat of her rubber bathing suit.

213. TA001-315 — Kern County Library / Taft Branch. Donor: James Turner.

214. SF-002-006 — San Francisco Public Library. Donor: Walter Deas.

215. TCS1-057 — Tulare County Library. Donor: Hiroshi Uota. (The Uota farm is also shown in 301.)

216. S-006-586 — Los Angeles Public Library. Donor: Sophie Tajima Toriumi. Left to right: Gohei Shoji, the Reverend Kengo Tajima, Helen Shoji, Sophie Tajima Toriumi, Kiyoko Shoji, Kobe Shoji.

217. PHO.99.Col.222-002 — Oakland Public Library. Donor: Darian Avelino.

218. SWAT-001-323 — Watsonville Public Library. Donor: Gabriela Hernandez. Fausto Romero was Gabriela's father.

219. PHO.99.Col.201-011 — Oakland Public Library. Donor: Kathy Sloane.

220. TCS1-085 — Tulare County Library. Donors: Tulare Historical Museum, Ling Joe family.

221. RCH-222 — Richmond Public Library. Donor: Kashan (Thomas) Robinson. Betty Jean Stevenson and Kashan Thomas were best friends.

222. SF-002-017 — San Francisco Public Library. Donor: Walter Deas.

223. SW4-005 — Whittier Public Library. Donor: Caroline Pastrano Lozano.

224. SSB-0-300 — San Bernardino Public Library. Donor: Chris Shovey. Right: Richard Fair, the donor's son.

225. 98-06-002 — Madera County Library. Donors: Mr. and Mrs. Cecil Neely. The boys' grandmothers were sisters. Both families had come to California from Texas in the 1930s and moved to Madera in the early 1940s. The two men are still close friends.

226. SSB-0-208 — San Bernardino Public Library. Donor: Masako Hirata. Masako was a teacher for 37 years. She and Brenda are still good friends.

227. COR-98-SH240 — Corona Public Library. Donor: Frances Martinez. The Highlights — front row: Al Lopez, Frank Lopez, William Gonzales Jr., Robert Macias; drummer Danel Sandoval; back row: Frank Torres, Elsie Corral, Robert Cervantes, Joaquin Flores Jr., and Larry Mejia. This was a local band. According to the donor, "It was a good orchestra. Back in those days, the dances all had live music."

228. S-009-261 — Los Angeles Public Library. Donor: John and Alice Bozajian. Left to right: Peter Gamoian, Vanig Shagoian (playing the mandolin), Herbert Elmassian, Vahan Khorigian, Guy Chookoorian (playing the oud).

229. S-001-268 — Riverside Public Library. Donor: Sue Strickland. The guitar player in the center of the photo is the donor's son, Eric Strickland. "Up with People," a singing group made up of a succession of college students, performed around the world for 35 years.

230. S-001-641 — Riverside Public Library. Donor: Rose Medina. The donor's son Reuben (the baby in the picture) is enjoying his first mariachi band.

231. SW3-027 — Whittier Public Library. Donor: Phyllis Woods. Front row, fifth from left: Laverne Knox. Back row, fifth from left: Leland Hunnicutt. Back row, far right: Raymond Hunnicutt.

232. TA001-432 — Kern County Library / Taft Branch. Donor: Pete Gianopulos. This theater burned down three times between the time it was built (1920s) and the 1950s. It had to be closed and remodeled once more in the late 1960s, when it was discovered that asbestos had been used in the seats during the 1950 renovation.

233. PHO.99.Col.201-013 — Oakland Public Library. Donor: Kathy Sloane.

234. MTY-6050 — Monterey Public Library. Donor: Natalie Whitney. The photo shows local businessmen who started the Jazz Festival to promote tourism in Monterey. The only musician in the bunch is the sax player, John Coyle, who owned the local music store. Holding his ears at the left of the picture is the famous bandleader Woody Herman.

235. SW3-062 — Whittier Public Library. Donor: Madi Comfort. Joseph and Madi are shown here dancing on their wedding night to Jimmy Lunceford's band at the Plantation Club. Joseph, a bass player, played with Frank Sinatra, Nat King Cole, Lionel Hampton, Ella Fitzgerald, and Duke Ellington. Madi was the "Satin Doll" of Duke Ellington's song. She also appeared in movies.

236. LB008-191 — Long Beach Public Library. Donor: Gloria Keo. This was taken at the Lotus Festival in Los Angeles. Dancers are (left to right): Soven Yim, Cathlean Kim, Nite (last name unknown), Gloria Keo, Samosan Kung, Cindy (last name unknown), and Sambath Yim. This ancient dance was first danced in its present form in Battanbong, Cambodia, in 1918. It is danced at weddings, baptisms, and other celebrations to give the gods' blessings; flower petals are dropped into a chumpean (cup), symbolic of good wishes for life.

237. SSF-001-189 — South San Francisco Public Library. Donor: Celia Bronstein. Mrs. Bronstein's husband, Milton (right rear), was the organizer of this band, an outgrowth of their music store.

238. SB-000-043 — Berkeley Public Library / South Branch. Donor: Euradee Maybuce. The Maybuce girls danced through most of their childhood, proficient in both tap and ballet.

239. SW1-008 — Whittier Public Library. Donor: John Sanders.

240. KC-001-130 — Kern County Library / Frazier Park Branch. Donor: David Nelson.

241. SF-002-359 — San Francisco Public Library. Donor: Julie Collins. Giulia Fontana is holding baby Danny Fontana in the background. Caroline and George's father, Scott Newhall, was the innovative editor of the *San Francisco Chronicle* who brought to the paper its famous columnists Herb Caen, Art Hoppe, Stanton Delaplane, Charles McCabe, and others.

242. KC-001-435 — Kern County Library / Frazier Park Branch. Donor: Alma Newman.

243. TCS1-223 — Tulare County Library. Donor: Jacque Lovelady.

244. KC-001-424 — Kern County Library / Frazier Park Branch. Donor: Alma Newman. Frazier Park, a small, rural mountain community, was a summer resort for residents of Los Angeles for most of the first half of the twentieth century. Longtime resident Daisy Cuddy says, "The L.A. kids brought an element of Hollywood sophistication to Frazier Park."

245. PHO.99.Col.211-004 — Oakland Public Library. Donor: Raymond Holbert. Left to right: Virgil Epperson, Stephanie Garland, Sandy Tighelman.

246. 98-05-005 — Madera County Library. Donor: Linda Sitterding. According to the donor, her grandmother, Mrs. Ferguson, used to say that when she met her future husband, "I didn't think much of him. He was stuck on hisself."

247. MTY-6244 — Monterey Public Library. Donor: Angela McCurry. Angelo (also pictured in 312) and Ruth were introduced at a Valentine's Day dance because they were the only two not dancing. It was love at first sight. After a long, happy life together, Ruth died three years before Angelo. This photo, taken near the place of their first meeting, is on their joint headstone.

248. 98-001-507 — Escondido Public Library. Donor: Dorothy Tavui. According to the donor, the family sold liquor out of house in late thirties. The house was "in the country then." During WWII barracks were built nearby, and Irene turned the house into a café for the troops.

249. S-007-043 — Los Angeles Public Library. Donor: Glenda Ahhaitty. The Dentadales are shown attending the 1976 powwow of the American Indian Employee Association at Rockwell International.

250. PHO.99.Col.222-012 — Oakland Public Library. Donor: Darian Avelino.

251. FOL-98-012 — Folsom Public Library. Donor: Myrtle Davies.

252. SSF-001-061 — South San Francisco Public Library. Donor: Constance Vetter.

253. SF-002-329 — San Francisco Public Library. Donor: Caroline Mota.

254. SSF-001-201 — South San Francisco Public Library. Donor: Shirley Nichols.

255. S-012-171 — Los Angeles Public Library. Donor: Yvonne Ng.

256. S1371 — Riverside Public Library. Donor: Lori Sisquoc. The Indian Health Summer Campout provides cultural programs, such as this basketry class, for children from several Indian reservations in Riverside County.

257. RCH-002 — Richmond Public Library. Donor: Mary Tom Coe.

258. SW4-076 — Whittier Public Library. Donor: Ron Coppock Jr. Mothers and babies. Whittier, 1944.

259. SW4-038 — Whittier Public Library. Donors: Vivian and Robert Vellanoweth. The Vellanoweth family at the site of their new home. Whittier, 1959. Orange groves were removed to build the houses in this new subdivision.

260. KC-001-514 — Kern County Library / Frazier Park Branch. Donor: Carol Darling. The Darling and Nikkel children on Alcot Trail. Frazier Park, early 1950s.

261. LB008-039 — Long Beach Public Library. Donor: Judith Anne Lines-Stearns. Five generations of mothers and daughters. Long Beach, 1978. Left to right: Della Johns, Myrtle Choate, Catherine Lines, Amanda Baggett, Judith Baggett.

262. SSF-001-172 — South San Francisco Public Library. Donor: Giffra family. This photo of the Giffra family was taken to send to a sick grandmother in Italy. South San Francisco, 1921.

263. AN-001-837 — Anaheim Public Library. Donor: Frank and Mary Hirahara. George and Koto Hirahara with their infant son, Frank. Yakima, Washington, c. 1926. The family lived in Yakima before moving to Long Beach.

264. SF-002-633 — San Francisco Public Library. Donor: Mary Kerrigan. Ann Linn and her children: Walter, George, and Arthur. San Francisco, c. 1910. Mrs. Linn's husband, George Henry, was an ironworker who worked on Sather Gate at the University of California, Berkeley.

265. SW3-028 — Whittier Public Library. Donor: Phyllis Woods. The Hunt sisters. Whittier, 1920. Left to right: Eva Hunt, Iva Hunt Hunnicutt; Laurenna, Ethylyn, and Hattie Hunt. The Hunt sisters were granddaughters of Jonathan Bailey, one of the original Quaker founders of the city of Whittier. The photo was taken at or near the Bailey house on Camilla Street. Iva's granddaughter Phyllis remembers that when she was a girl, the older people still said "thee" and "thou" and that her grandmother was fond of this Quaker joke: "Everyone except me and thee is a little strange and sometimes I wonder about thee."

266. MTY-6453 — Monterey Public Library. Donor: Edward Elsen. Alphonse and Marie Elsen at home on Carmelito Circle. Monterey, c. 1921. Edward Elsen (the donor's grandfather) built this house for his bride, Philomena. Their children, Alphonse and Marie, were born here. Edward owned a candy and ice cream store on the Monterey wharf.

267. 98-06-11B — Madera County Library. Donor: Maxine A. Holmes. Grace Arnold at home at the Sharon Home Ranch. Madera, 1960s.

268. S-01-123 — Sutter County Library. Donor: Balbir (Rai) Dhaddey. The Sohar Singh Rai family. Yuba City, c. 1961. Left to right: Sarnjit, Balbir, Sohan, Kuldip, Joginder, and Amerjit Singh Rai. Kuldip, then twelve, won the portrait by giving the correct answer to the question "What is the capital of California?" on a radio contest.

269. SW2-007 — Whittier Public Library. Donor: Marlene Martel. The Rowe family at Whittier city yard. Whittier, 1954. Left to right: Thelma Rowe, baby Marilyn Mendez, Joan Mendez, Charlotte Rowe, Charles Rowe, Marvin Mendez. Charles was captain in the Whittier Fire Department for 26 years. This picture was taken at the fire station. Asked if her grandmother worried about Charles being a fireman, Marlene said, "Grandma had confidence in him and didn't worry too much."

270. 98-02-059 — Madera County Library. Donor: Frank Neufeld. The family fled Russia, crossing the Amur River into China in a hail of bullets. They came to the United States in 1933. The donor and his five brothers (all in this photograph) were all in the U.S. Army and all survived the war. Back row, left to right, capped: David, paratrooper and demolition specialist; John, infantry, jeep driver, and interpreter; Bill, infantry; Abe, infantry and artillery; Jack, intelligence and interpreter; and Frank, infantry and surgical nurse.

271. PHO.99.Col.212-011 — Oakland Public Library. Donor: Rhonda White-Warner.

272. AN-001-617 — Anaheim Public Library. Donor: Lupe E. Reyes. The family had gone to Grandma's house to help her in her garden. After a day spent working in the dirt, they put all the kids in the bathtub. Frank and Sally decided to celebrate the phenomenon of having all four young children clean at the same time by taking the photograph. Left to right, the girls are Annie, Lupe, Ramona, and Rose.

273. SB-000-594 — Berkeley Public Library / South Branch. Donor: Charmaine Steven.

274. S-01-206 — Sutter County Library. Donor: Gina McRunnels. Tomasina was from Jalisco, Mexico. The Valdez family moved to Sutter County in 1940.

275. 98-06-30 — Madera County Library. Donor: Dorothy Firmalo Tigson. John Firmalo, a native of the Philippines, had been a U.S. Navy steward in WWI. He met his future wife while both were working for Patrick Roberts in Madera. They married over the objections of Alice's parents, who relented years later when a visiting relative told them of John's devotion to his family. John Firmalo died in September 1941, and early the next year his widow, who had been born in Hawaii to Japanese parents, was interned with her seven children in the Fresno Assembly Center at the Fresno fairgrounds. Dorothy graduated from high school while in the camp.

276. 98-001-318 — Escondido Public Library. Donor: James Bulen Jr.

277. AN-001-519 — Anaheim Public Library. Donor: Francisca Provencio.

278. SSF-001-010 — South San Francisco Public Library. Donor: George Bugnatto.

279. PHO.99.Col.200-002 — Oakland Public Library. Donor: Mary Ellen Butler. Mary Ellen says, "I always hated to have my picture taken."

280. SSB-0-036 — San Bernardino Public Library. Donor: Luna Aurora.

281. KC-001-030 — Kern County Library / Frazier Park Branch. Donor: Sean Malis. The boy in the rear of the picture, Robert Hallowell Gardiner IV, later became a governor of Massachusetts.

282. SSF-001-260 — South San Francisco Public Library. Donor: Sylvia Payne. This photo is the donor's favorite from her campaign brochure. She successfully ran for South San Francisco city clerk in 1985.

283. KC-001-255 — Kern County Library / Frazier Park Branch. Donor: Gloria Cuddy. The "Cuddy Place" was used for exterior shots of the home on the 1970s television show *The Waltons.*

284. TCS1-009 — Tulare County Library. Donor: Jun Hatakeda. Hatsuye is the donor's sister.

285. FOL-98-331 — Folsom Public Library. Donor: Elizabeth Moore. Left to right: Mary Purcell, Larry Purcell, Cecilia Moore, Helen Purcell. Mrs. Purcell was the donor's mother. Her father was a prison guard and the family lived on the prison grounds. The photo was taken by Joe Rosenthal, who took the famous photo of Marines raising the American flag on Iwo Jima.

286. S-01-439 — Sutter County Library. Donor: Judy Hale.

287. SSF-001-180 — South San Francisco Public Library. Donor: Delphine Carter.

288. TCS1-225 — Tulare County Library. Donor: Jacque Lovelady. Ling Joe's birth name was Ling Haw. He had an early business partner surnamed Joe. When Mr. Joe left, townspeople were unable to sort out the two names and thus Ling Haw became Ling Joe. Most Chinese were driven from Tulare County about the time this photo was taken. Ling Joe was permitted to remain, perhaps because he owned a popular restaurant where he served "American" food.

289. TCS1-086 — Tulare County Library. Donors: Tulare Historical Museum, Ling Joe family.

290. TCS1-091 — Tulare County Library. Donors: Tulare Historical Museum, Ling Joe family. Left to right: Mary Joe (Mrs. Ling Joe), her son Yow Joe (also pictured in 220), David Haw (Yow Joe's son), Bing (the chef, last name unknown), and Wing Wong (Mary Joe's grandson). Because of Mary Joe's generosity to the railroad hobos, a family friend warned her against becoming known as an easy mark. Mary thanked him and replied, "Pops, better to give to all than to miss one who needs it."

291. S-01-167 — Sutter County Library. Donor: Katy Lim. This was the first Chinese couple to be married in an airplane. The bride, Alice Lee, was Katy's babysitter and, as it turned out, also her aunt. Katy had lost her mother at an early age and had no idea that Alice was her aunt. Alice's husband discovered the relationship after Alice's death and gave Katy this photo.

292. 98-05-037 — Madera County Library. Donor: Mary Pehl. The donor's parents are accompanied by Jose Morales, the best man, and Elena Acuña, the maid of honor. (Gilbert Fimbrez also appears in 188.)

293. LB008-116 — Long Beach Public Library. Donor: Connie Williams.

294. S-01-102 — Sutter County Library. Donor: Linda Valdez.

295. 98-03-018 — Fresno County Library. Donor: Diana Bell.

The three-day wedding celebration is in the Volga-German tradition. These were Germans who lived in Russia and then emigrated to the United States.

296. SW1-007 — Whittier Public Library. Donor: John Sanders. Left to right: Rosa Lee Ramirez, Henry Ramirez (rear), John Darius, Laura Ramirez.

297. S1083 — Riverside Public Library. Donor: Suma Hareesh. The donor's daughters had their hands decorated with henna (Mehendi) for a wedding.

298. PHO.99.Col.237-014 — Oakland Public Library. Donor: Audrey Robinson.

299. COR-98-SH256 — Corona Public Library. Donor: Frances Martinez.

300. LB008-219 — Long Beach Public Library. Donor: Linda Tovar Garza.

301. TCS1-457 — Tulare County Library. Donor: Baron Nitta.

302. TA001-029 — Kern County Library / Taft Branch. Donor: Robert LeGar.

303. HU-000-083 — Humboldt County Library. Donor: Isaac Moxon. There were once 154 dairies in Humboldt County. There are now only eight or nine left.

304. SSB-0-315 — San Bernardino Public Library. Donor: August Santini. Feeding the cows on his father's dairy farm was one of August's many morning chores.

305. TCS1-460 — Tulare County Library. Donor: Gayle Kajioka. Alice Suyeda (also pictured in 178) is the donor's mother; Nancy Morioka is her aunt. Kinuyo Morioka (on left) and Yoshikazu Morioka are in the background.

306. HU-000-450 — Humboldt County Library. Donors: Francis C. and Sylvia S. White. Emil Frey, a dairy farmer, came from Switzerland and married Annie, a Yurok woman. Minnie Swan was half Yurok. She and Emil were fishing buddies.

307. LB008-176 — Long Beach Public Library. Donor: Floris Tyner. Commercial fishermen loaded huge nets into boats, rowed out, and laid the nets in a loop. They anchored one end of the nets onshore, then hooked the other end to a team of horses, which brought in the nets. The fish were taken by wagon to trains in Long Beach and then shipped to Los Angeles.

308. AN-001-530 — Anaheim Public Library. Donor: Saturnino Muro.

309. HU-000-408I — Humboldt County Library. Donor: Susan Sanders.

310. COR-98-SH211 — Corona Public Library. Donor: Cathy Salgado Blankenbeker.

311. S-001-203 — Riverside Public Library. Donors: Manuel and Mary Blunt.

312. MTY-6233 — Monterey Public Library. Donor: Angela McCurry. Joseph Anastasia came to New Jersey from Sicily in the early part of the twentieth century to work in the cotton mills. He hated the work and had always wanted to be a fisherman, so he moved to Monterey, where he caught fish and peddled them on the wharf, eventually building up the business into Anastasia's Fish Market.

313. SSF-001-220 — South San Francisco Public Library. Donors: Bob and Helen Penna.

314. MTY-6804 — Monterey Public Library. Donor: Jeanne McCombs. The Thornburgs, left to right: Luella, Sam (proprietor), Delia, Edward, and Edith.

315. SF-002-233 — San Francisco Public Library. Donor: Lorraine Hazen.

316. TA001-318 — Kern County Library / Taft Branch. Donor: Kathleen Grantham.

317. SF-002-600 — San Francisco Public Library. Donor: Joseph Anmuth. Johny, second from left, was very popular during the depression because he let people eat at his restaurant on credit if they couldn't pay.

318. 98-02-035 — Fresno County Library. Donor: Diana Bell.

319. RCH-345 — Richmond Public Library. Donor: Kathleen Rupley. Left to right: Monica Soby, Patricia Rupley, Edith Crough. It was customary for the women to finish the contents of the "Earl of Manhattan" pitcher while cleaning up.

320. AN-001-303 — Anaheim Public Library. Donor: Robert Takazumi. The squid barbecue was a fundraiser for the Manshiko Club, a group of Japanese Americans who meet at the local Buddhist church.

321. SSF-001-006 — South San Francisco Public Library. Donor: George Bugnatto. Left to right: Margarite Bugnatto, John Carly, Audrey Carly, Peter Bugnatto, Elsie Carly, an unidentified woman.

322. MTY-6440 — Monterey Public Library. Donor: Ann Todd. Left to right: Clarence Goldsworthy, Ted McKay, Roland Ingles, Robert McKever Jr., Sal Cerito. The donor knew that the anniversary party for her grandparents was a success: "the guests were falling over into the bushes as they left."

323. MTY-6218 — Monterey Public Library. Donor: Jeannie Cordero. The Piazzoni family had many big barbecues; Luigi made his own sausage and wine. The women in the picture, Luigi's daughter Helen and one of her seven sisters, were enthusiastic horsewomen who rode everywhere, even on their errands into town. Luigi's wife, Tomasa Manjarez, was an Esselen Indian. The family enjoyed their own informal rodeos at the ranch. Helen could rope and ride with the best of them. Left to right: A Piazzoni sister, Helen Piazzoni, two neighbors, Luigi Piazzoni.

324. SSF-001-058 — South San Francisco Public Library. Donor: Paul Tognetti. Left to right around the table: Pete Durigano, Jim Christensen, Dekin Jemas, Dr. Stimer, Albert Tognetti, Angelo (last name unknown), Paul Tognetti. High bet was a nickel.

325. SW1-065 — Whittier Public Library. Donor: Lisa Gonzalez. The kids in the picture really did hunt two-week-old eggs, to celebrate belatedly with friends.

326. PHO.99.Col.201-008 — Oakland Public Library. Donor: Kathy Sloane. Left to right: Delores Holder, Neddie Sloane, Anne Maria Hardeman, Renee Boone.

327. SSF-001-045 — South San Francisco Public Library. Donor: Paul Tognetti. The little boy in the background, Bruce Tognetti, later became Colma's chief of police.

328. RCH-010 — Richmond Public Library. Donors: Mary and Tom Coe. The bride and groom and their guests, Jinx Wood, Dorothy Bergland, Francis Shelton, and Jeanice Shelton, were leaving for the Claremont Hotel in Berkeley to celebrate after the evening wedding at Thousand Oaks Baptist Church. Their honeymoon suite at the Claremont cost five dollars.

329. TA001-047 — Kern County Library / Taft Branch. Donor: Pete Gianopulos. Mr. and Mrs. Frank Panusis on a Sunday picnic at the Maricopa flats with Vasiliki Gianopulos and her children. Taft, c. 1935. The Panusis children are Fred and Charles. The Gianopulos children are Margaret, George, and Pete. Their father, Tom Gianopulos (also in 340), took the picture. Pete is a past mayor of Taft and the local historian.

330. L A.S-012-629 — Los Angeles Public Library. Donor: Mary Buckley. Linda Buckley's birthday party. Panorama City, 1958. Left to right: Sheila Brason, Linda Buckley, Kathy Miller, and Mary Buckley.

331. SSB-0-410 — San Bernardino Public Library. Donor: Robert Stanton. Robert Stanton's school birthday party. San Bernardino, c. 1930.

332. S-001-629 — Riverside Public Library. Donor: Rose Medina. Christmas with Michael. Moreno Valley, 1996. Michael owned the China Garden Restaurant. He always came to the Lopez's for Christmas and he always carved the turkey because he was so good at it.

333. SSB-0-403 — San Bernardino Public Library. Donor: Henry Hooks. The Lily of the Valley Eastern Star Chapter 12 holds a tea party at the Masonic Hall. San Bernardino, 1952. Left to right: Opal L. Hooks, Thomas Andrews, Alice York, Ussie L. Andrews, Richard Patterson, Naoma McDuff, Marie Muchleroy, Katherine Elmre, Lititia Ingraham.

334. S-001-202 — Riverside Public Library. Donors: Manuel and Mary Blunt. Camacho and Jesus Gonzalez at work in the Jameson packing house. Riverside, early 1940s.

335. SSB-0-240 — San Bernardino Public Library. Donor: Penny Holcomb. A "watermelon orgy" at the Holcomb family picnic. Cedar Pines Park, Crestline, 1958. The photo shows the donor's children and their friends, Jay Holcomb, Steve Fich, Terri Lee Holcomb, Bill Holcomb, Bill Eich. Terri's brothers took her name from the comic strip "Terry and the Pirates" and her parents feminized it.

336. S-01-539 — Sutter County Library. Donor: Nenita Smith. The Smiths' Christmas dinner party. Yuba City, 1997.

337. SSF-001-070 — South San Francisco Public Library. Donor: Dory Cocadiz. A Cocadiz family celebration. South San Francisco, c. 1997. The donor can't remember what occasion the family was celebrating: "We roast pigs all the time."

338. SB-000-151 — Berkeley Public Library / South Branch. Donor: David Reid. "The Soiree" for Alpha Kappa Alpha, at the International House in Berkeley, c. 1950. Left to right: unknown, Melvin Reid, Betty Charbonnet Reid.

339. SSB-0-309 — San Bernardino Public Library. Donor: Joel Martin Jr. The donor is shown on the running board of the Arrowhead Ice Cream truck in front of the Candy Kitchen in San Bernardino, 1923. Joel Martin Sr. owned a candy store until the earthquake of 1924. The family lived above the store. Joel Sr. made braided baskets out of hard candy. His formulas were in code and the recipes were lost when he died.

340. TA001-428 — Kern County Library / Taft Branch. Donor: Pete Gianopulos. The Westside Fruit Company, c. 1922. Owners Tom Gianopulos and Tony Harris are on the left and right. Taft, c. 1922. Tom Gianopulos was the donor's father.

341. SSF-001-269 — South San Francisco Public Library. Donor: Irene Chagaris.

342. SF-001-654 — San Francisco Public Library. Donor: Nobu Mihara.

343. SW2-008 — Whittier Public Library. Donor: Marlene Martel.

344. SB-000-465 — Berkeley Public Library / South Branch. Donor: Mary Trahan. The girls camped in various places around California throughout their childhood. When they couldn't camp, they roasted marshmallows on the stove in the Wiggins's kitchen.

345. KC-001-225 — Kern County Library / Frazier Park Branch. Donor: Nancy Kashanski. Nancy took this photograph of her children.

346. SF-002-708 — San Francisco Public Library. Donor: Ron Sullivan. Rear, left to right: Mr. Personini holding his grandson Joey; his daughter-in-law Julia; an unidentified man holding a baby; Dolores Slattery. Front: George Personini (Julia's husband); the donor; his father, Fred Sullivan; his mother, Mary Slattery Sullivan.

347. SW5-043 — Whittier Public Library. Donor: Jan Lopez. Jan made her dress and the bridesmaid's dress. Jan and Vic squeezed orange juice for the punch; friends donated flowers. Jan later made her daughters' wedding dresses. Victor was the first Mexican American mayor of Whittier, and the first Mexican American allowed to buy a house in Whittier.

348. KC-001-248 — Kern County Library / Frazier Park Branch. Donor: Gloria Cuddy. Charles F. Cuddy, who died later that year, said of this photo: "This is how I want to be remembered." Frazier Park, 1989.

349. Donor: Los Angeles Public Library. Louise and Woona Park at the Korean Photo Day, Los Angeles, October 3, 1992.

350. Donor: Los Angeles Public Library. African American Photo Day at the Museum of African American Art, Los Angeles, November 2, 1991.

351. Donor: Pete Gianopulos. The photo shows Pete Gianopulos and Robert and Karen Mitchell at the "Shades of the West Side" Exhibit, Kern County Library, Taft Branch, September 13, 1999.

352. Donor: Los Angeles Public Library. Left to right: Shades of L.A. photographers Coleman Grimmette and Bob Douglas, Los Angeles, c. 1991.

353. Donor: Los Angeles Public Library. Photo Day at the Western Addition Branch Library, San Francisco, March 29, 1998.

354–365. See next two pages.

366. S-012-142 — Los Angeles Public Library. Donor: Helena Hofmanis. The donor's father, Aleksandrs Nuksa, was making a self-portrait when Helena walked in and asked, "Hey, Papa, what are you doing?"

354

355

356

357

354. Right to left: Jeannine Gendar [managing editor] with her mother, Carolyn Dando (Gendar) Pearce, her grandmother Muriel Proper Dando, and her great-grandmother Alice Clark Proper. Sherman Oaks, 1950.
355. Robert Daseler [author of the introduction] photographing his son, Chase. Sausalito, c. 1992. **356.** Kathy Kobayashi [co-author of the afterword] with her brother, John, and their grandparents, Moto and Mitsutaro Kobayashi. Webster, Texas, 1954. **357.** Left to right: Kimi Kodani Hill [photo editor] pretending to read to John Prowdy, Kei Kodani, David Wilson, and Kirk Westfall. Oakland, c. 1962. **358.** Laura (Brenkwitz) Kennedy [editorial assistant] and her brother, Stephen Brenkwitz. Tracy, late 1950s. **359.** Graham Daseler, Robert's son. Claremont, 1988.

358

359

360

361

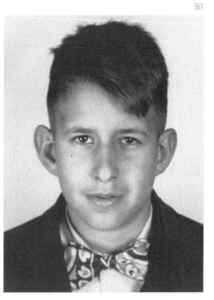

363

362

360. Rebecca LeGates [production manager] at her grandparents' home. Sarasota, Florida, 1977. **361.** Malcolm Margolin [publisher of Heyday Books]. Boston, Massachusetts, c. 1950. **362.** Left to right: Doug Wakida [research assistant] with his cousin, Kellee Verhaert, and his sister Patricia Wakida [project director], in their grandparents' bathtub. Sanger, c. 1977. **363.** David Bullen [designer] with his father, Reese Bullen, at their home. Arcata, the late 1950s. **364.** Carolyn Kozo Cole [co-author of the afterword] with her great-grandmother Matilda Greschel Anderson, her mother, June Smith Jennings (left, standing), and her grandmother Hertha Smith (right, standing). Fredericksburg, Virginia, 1947. **365.** Ken Sanderson [research assistant]. Fort Bragg, 1971.

364

365